First World War
and Army of Occupation
War Diary
France, Belgium and Germany

4 CAVALRY DIVISION
Divisional Troops
Royal Army Medical Corps
Combined Cavalry Field Ambulance Sialkot, Mhow and Lucknow
1 January 1917 - 31 March 1918

WO95/1158/6

The Naval & Military Press Ltd
www.nmarchive.com
Published in association with The National Archives

Published by

The Naval & Military Press Ltd

Unit 10 Ridgewood Industrial Park,

Uckfield, East Sussex,

TN22 5QE England

Tel: +44 (0) 1825 749494

www.naval-military-press.com

www.nmarchive.com

This diary has been reprinted in facsimile from the original. Any imperfections are inevitably reproduced and the quality may fall short of modern type and cartographic standards.

© **Crown Copyright**
Images reproduced by permission of The National Archives, London, England, 2015.

Contents

Document type	Place/Title	Date From	Date To
Heading	WO95/1158/6		
Heading	4 Cav Div Troops Combined Field Ambulance Lucknow Mhow Sialkot 1917 Jan-1918 Apr		
Heading	B E F 4 Cav Div. Troops Lucknow Cav Fld Amb 1917 Jan To 1918 Feb To Egypt 4 Cav Div		
Heading	War Diary of Lucknow Cavalry Field Ambulance.-4th. Cavalry Division From 1st January 1917. To 31st January 1917		
War Diary	Acheux	02/01/1917	30/01/1917
Heading	War Diary of Lucknow Cav Field Ambulance From 1-2-17 To 28-2-17 Volume XXVII		
War Diary	Acheux	02/02/1917	26/02/1917
Heading	War Diary of Lucknow. Cav. Field. Ambulance from 1-3-17 to 31-3-17 vol XXVIII		
War Diary	Acheux	02/03/1917	17/03/1917
War Diary	Millencourt	19/03/1917	19/03/1917
War Diary	Franqueville	20/03/1917	20/03/1917
War Diary	Albert-Aveluy Rd.	21/03/1917	30/03/1917
Heading	War Diary of Lucknow Cav. Field Ambulance from 1-4-17 to 30-4-17 Vol XXVIII		
War Diary	Albert-Aveluy Rd.	01/04/1917	07/04/1917
War Diary	Irles	08/04/1917	12/04/1917
War Diary	Aveluy	13/04/1917	13/04/1917
War Diary	Bus-Les-Artois	14/04/1917	30/04/1917
Heading	War Diary of Lucknow Cavalry Field Ambulance from 1-5-17 to 31-5-17 Vol XXIX		
War Diary	Bus-Les-Artois	01/05/1917	14/05/1917
War Diary	Meault	15/05/1917	15/05/1917
War Diary	Suzanne	16/05/1917	16/05/1917
War Diary	St Cren	17/05/1917	30/05/1917
Heading	War Diary of Lucknow C. F. A from 1-6-17 to 30-6-17 Vol XXIX		
War Diary	St Cren	01/06/1917	30/06/1917
Heading	War Diary of Lucknow C. F. A from 1-7-17 to 31-7-17 Vol XXX		
War Diary	S. Cren	01/07/1917	31/07/1917
Heading	War Diary of Lucknow Cavalry Field Ambulance from 1-8-17 to 31-8-17 Vol XXXI		
War Diary	St Cren	01/08/1917	05/08/1917
War Diary	St Christ	06/08/1917	31/08/1917
Heading	War Diary of Lucknow Cav Fd. Amb. from 1-9-17 to 30-9-17 Vol XXXII		
War Diary	St Christ	01/09/1917	30/09/1917
Heading	War Diary of Lucknow Cav Fd Ambulance from 1-10-17 to 31-10-17 Vol XXXIII		
War Diary	St Christ	01/10/1917	30/10/1917
Heading	War Diary of Lucknow Cavalry Field Ambulance from 1-11-17 to 30-11-17 Vol XXXIV		
War Diary	St Christ	03/11/1917	18/11/1917
War Diary	Longavesne	19/11/1917	20/11/1917

War Diary	Fins	21/11/1917	22/11/1917
War Diary	Fourques	23/11/1917	28/11/1917
War Diary	Villers-Faucon	30/11/1917	30/11/1917
Heading	War Diary of Lucknow Cavalry Field Ambulance for month of December 1917. Volume. XXXV		
War Diary	Villers-Faucon	01/12/1917	02/12/1917
War Diary	Le Mesnil	03/12/1917	18/12/1917
War Diary	St Cren	20/12/1917	31/12/1917
Heading	Lucknow Cav. F. Ambce.		
Heading	War Diary of Lucknow Cavalry Field Ambulance for month of January 1918. Volume XXXVI		
War Diary	St Cren	01/01/1918	31/01/1918
Heading	War Diary of Lucknow Cavalry Field Ambulance for month of February 1918 Volume XXXVII		
War Diary	St Cren	01/02/1918	04/02/1918
War Diary	Marcelcave	06/02/1918	06/02/1918
War Diary	Namps-Au-Mont	07/02/1918	28/02/1918
Heading	1918 4th Cavalry Division 104 Mhow Cavalry Fld Ambs Jan-Apl 19181917 Feb 1918 Mar To Egypt 1 Mounted Div Troops		
Heading	Sialkot Mhow Lucknow Cav. Fd. Ambs.		
Heading	Mhow Cav. Field Ambulance 5th Cav. Division. Feb 1917		
Heading	Mhow Indian Cavalry Field Ambulance from 1st to 28th February 1917.		
War Diary	Bouvaincourt	01/02/1917	28/02/1917
Heading	Mhow Cav. F. A. Mar 1917		
War Diary	Bouvaincourt	01/03/1917	19/03/1917
War Diary	Senarpont	20/03/1917	20/03/1917
War Diary	Revelles	21/03/1917	21/03/1917
War Diary	Cachy	22/03/1917	22/03/1917
War Diary	Bois De Mereaucourt	23/03/1917	23/03/1917
War Diary	Prusles	24/03/1917	28/03/1917
War Diary	Bois De Mereaucourt	29/03/1917	29/03/1917
War Diary	Warfusee Abaincourt	30/03/1917	31/03/1917
Heading	Mhow. Cav. F. A. April 1917		
War Diary	Warfusee-Abaincourt	01/04/1917	13/04/1917
War Diary	Coulaincourt	14/04/1917	30/04/1917
Heading	Mhow Ind. Cav. Field Ambulance. May 1917		
War Diary	Coulaincourt	01/05/1917	31/05/1917
Miscellaneous	Canadian C.F.A. Appendix I		
Miscellaneous	Situation of other Medical Units. Appendix II		
Miscellaneous	Appendix III		
Miscellaneous	Medical Arrangements to C A V: Corps Appendix IV		
Miscellaneous	Copy of D.D.M.S. Cav. Corps No. M/10/8 & 25.5.17 Appendix V		
Heading	Mhow Indian Cav. F. A. June 1917		
War Diary	Caulaincourt. 1/20,000 Sheet 62c S.E W. 5a 5.5.	01/06/1917	05/06/1917
War Diary	Caulaincourt	06/06/1917	30/06/1917
Miscellaneous	Dental Centre, Tincourt. Two Dental Surgeon. (Nos 5 & 36 C.C.S.)		
Miscellaneous	All Officers, N.C.Os. and men reporting as:- Appendix III		
Miscellaneous	Advanced Dressing Section. Appendix II		
Heading	Mhow Ind. Cav. F. A. July 1917		

Heading	Mhow Indian Cavalry Field Ambulance. from 1st to 31st July 1917		
Miscellaneous	Correspondence received General's Base Office.		
War Diary	Caulaincourt	01/07/1917	06/07/1917
War Diary	Caulaincourt Tertry	07/07/1917	07/07/1917
War Diary	Tertry	08/07/1917	12/07/1917
War Diary	Cartigny	13/07/1917	13/07/1917
War Diary	Suzanne	14/07/1917	14/07/1917
War Diary	Morlancourt	15/07/1917	15/07/1917
War Diary	Marieux	16/07/1917	16/07/1917
War Diary	St Michel	17/07/1917	31/07/1917
Miscellaneous	Appendix I		
Heading	Mhow Cav. F. A. Aug 1917		
Heading	Mhow Cavalry Field Ambulance From 1st to 31st August 1917.		
War Diary	St Michel	01/08/1917	31/08/1917
Heading	104th (Mhow) Ind. Cav. F. A. Sept 1917		
War Diary	St Michel	01/09/1917	30/09/1917
Heading	Mhow Cav. F. A. Oct 1917		
War Diary	St Michel	01/10/1917	06/10/1917
War Diary	Thiennes	07/10/1917	10/10/1917
War Diary	K 16 d 9. 8. 1/40,000 Sheet 27.	11/10/1917	13/10/1917
War Diary	Banderinghem	14/10/1917	14/10/1917
War Diary	Williametz	15/10/1917	15/10/1917
War Diary	Contes 1/100,000 Abbeville Sheet 14.	16/10/1917	19/10/1917
War Diary	Contes	20/10/1917	31/10/1917
Miscellaneous	Fallowing are Medical arrangements to on arriving in second Army area, they with come into force from, noon October 7th:- Appendix I	04/10/1917	04/10/1917
Miscellaneous	The following Location of medical units in the area are forwarded for informations:- Appendix II	08/10/1917	08/10/1917
Miscellaneous	Appendix III	09/10/1917	09/10/1917
Miscellaneous	Appendix IV	14/10/1917	14/10/1917
Miscellaneous	The following will be the arrangements for evacuation of seek in this area:- Appendix V	16/10/1917	16/10/1917
Miscellaneous	The following will be the medical arrangement While in this Area:- Appendix VI	19/10/1917	19/10/1917
Heading	Mhow Cav. F. A. Nov 1917		
War Diary	Contes	01/11/1917	08/11/1917
War Diary	Remaisnil	09/11/1917	09/11/1917
War Diary	Behencourt	10/11/1917	10/11/1917
War Diary	Suzanne	11/11/1917	11/11/1917
War Diary	Cartigny	12/11/1917	19/11/1917
War Diary	Near Fins	20/11/1917	20/11/1917
War Diary	K 30. d. 9.	21/11/1917	21/11/1917
War Diary	Equancourt	22/11/1917	22/11/1917
War Diary	Etinehem	23/11/1917	26/11/1917
War Diary	Tertry	27/11/1917	30/11/1917
War Diary	Villers Faucon	30/11/1917	30/11/1917
Miscellaneous	Extract from Operation Order Medical No 11 Appendix No I	08/11/1917	08/11/1917
Miscellaneous	The following are the arrangements for evacuation of seek etc while in this area. Appendix No. 2.		
Miscellaneous	Extract from Operation Order Medical No.12 Appendix No. 3.	18/11/1917	18/11/1917
Miscellaneous	Appendix No. 4.		

Heading	104 Mhow Ind. Cav. F. A. Dec 1917		
War Diary	Sheet 57 C 1/40,000 Villers Faucon	01/12/1917	02/12/1917
War Diary	Villers Faucon	03/12/1917	07/12/1917
War Diary	Brusle	08/12/1917	22/12/1917
War Diary	Tertry	23/12/1917	31/12/1917
Heading	104th Mhow Ind. Cav. F. A. Jan 1918		
War Diary	Tertry	01/01/1918	25/01/1918
War Diary	Bihecourt Station R 20 d 9-4	26/01/1918	31/01/1918
Miscellaneous	Table of duties of Brigades Appendix No I		
Miscellaneous	Extract from Cavalry Corps Medical arrangements Operations No 19 dated 14th Dec. 1917 map Reference 62c 1/40,000 Appendix No II		
Miscellaneous	Extract from 5th Cav: Div: Operation Order Medical No: 14 Appendix III		
Miscellaneous	List of Personnel Appendix IV		
Heading	War Diary of (Unit) 104th (Mhow) Cav. Field Ambulance E. E. Force. (Period) 1st February 1918. To 28th February 1918. Volume XL		
War Diary	20 1/40.000 Bihecourt Station R. 20 d 4.9	01/02/1918	08/02/1918
War Diary	Bihecourt Station R. 20 d 4.9	09/02/1918	16/02/1918
War Diary	Yaucourt Bussus (Abbeville 1/100,00)	17/02/1918	22/02/1918
War Diary	Yaucourt Bussus	23/02/1918	26/02/1918
War Diary	Migny Miens 1.00.000	27/02/1918	28/02/1918
Operation(al) Order(s)	Vault Operation Order No. 1.	11/02/1918	11/02/1918
Miscellaneous	Appendix II		
Miscellaneous	Appendix III	12/09/1918	12/09/1918
Heading	War Diary of (Unit) 104th (Mhow) Ind. Cav. Field Ambulance E. E. Force. (Period) 1st March 1918. To 31st March 1918. Volume XLI		
War Diary	Rumigny	01/03/1918	01/03/1918
War Diary	Saleux	02/03/1918	04/03/1918
War Diary	Marseilles	05/03/1918	31/03/1918
Heading	B D F 4 Cav Div Troops Sialcot Cav Fld Amb 1917 Jan To 1918 Apl To Egypt 4 Cav. Div Troops		
Heading	War Diary of Sialkot Cavalry Field Ambulance. 4th Cavalry Division From 1st January 1917. To 31st January 1917.		
War Diary	Meaulte	01/01/1917	12/01/1917
War Diary	Boubert	13/01/1917	31/01/1917
Heading	War Diary of Sialkote Cavalry Field Ambulance From 1.2.17 to 28.2.17 Vol XXV		
War Diary	Boubert	01/02/1917	25/02/1917
War Diary	Wargnies	26/02/1917	28/02/1917
Heading	War Diary of Sialkot Cavalry Field Ambulance From 1.3.17 to 31.3.17 Vol XXVI		
War Diary	Albert	01/03/1917	03/03/1917
War Diary	St. Ouen	04/03/1917	17/03/1917
War Diary	Aveluy	18/03/1917	18/03/1917
War Diary	Achiet Le Grand	19/03/1917	19/03/1917
War Diary	Bihucourt	20/03/1917	25/03/1917
War Diary	Irles	26/03/1917	29/03/1917
Heading	War Diary of Sialkot. C.F.A. From 1.4.17 to 30.4.17 Vol XXVII		
War Diary	Irles	01/04/1917	05/04/1917
War Diary	Bihucourt	06/04/1917	13/04/1917
War Diary	Aveluy	14/04/1917	24/04/1917

War Diary	Couin	25/04/1917	30/04/1917
War Diary	Irles	29/03/1917	31/03/1917
Heading	War Diary of Sialkote Cavalry Field Ambulance From 1.5.17 to 31.5.17 Vol XXVIII		
War Diary	Couin	01/05/1917	14/05/1917
War Diary	Ville Sous Corbie	15/05/1917	15/05/1917
War Diary	Maurepas	16/05/1917	16/05/1917
War Diary	Fourques	17/05/1917	31/05/1917
Heading	War Diary of Sialkot Cavalry Field Ambulance From 1.6.17 to 30.6.17 Vol. XXIX		
War Diary	Fourques	01/06/1917	30/06/1917
Heading	War Diary of Sialkot Cavalry Field Ambulance From 1.7.17 to 31.7.17 Vol. XXX		
War Diary	Fourques	01/07/1917	31/07/1917
Heading	War Diary of Sialkot Cavalry Field Ambulance From 1.8.17 to 31.8.17 Vol XXXI		
War Diary	Fourques	01/08/1917	05/08/1917
War Diary	St Cren	06/08/1917	31/08/1917
Heading	War Diary of Sialkot Cavalry Field Ambulance From 1.9.17 to 30.9.17 Vol. XXXII		
War Diary	St. Cren	01/09/1917	30/09/1917
Heading	War Diary of Sialkot Cavalry Field Ambulance From 1.10.17 to 31.10.17 Vol. XXXIII		
War Diary	St Cren	01/10/1917	31/10/1917
Heading	War Diary of Sialkot Cavalry Field Ambulance From 1.11.17 to 30.11.17 Vol XXXIV		
War Diary	St Cren	01/11/1917	20/11/1917
War Diary	Fins	21/11/1917	22/11/1917
War Diary	St Christ	23/11/1917	30/11/1917
Heading	War Diary of Sialkot Cav Field Ambulance From 1.12.17 to 31.12.17 Vol. XXXV		
War Diary	Villers Faucon	01/12/1917	02/12/1917
War Diary	St Christ	03/12/1917	31/12/1917
Heading	War Diary of Sialkot Cav. Field Ambulance To 1.1.18 from 31.1.18 Vol XXXVI		
War Diary	St Christ	01/01/1918	31/01/1918
Heading	War Diary of Sialkot Cav. Field Ambulance From 1.2.18 to 28.2.18 Vol XXXVII		
War Diary	Field.	01/02/1918	28/02/1918
Heading	Sialkot Cav. F. A. March 1918		
Heading	War Diary of Sialkot Cav. Field Ambulance From 1.3.18 to 31.2.18 Vol XXXVIII		
War Diary	Field (Marsielles)	01/03/1918	07/03/1918
War Diary	At Sea.	08/03/1918	14/03/1918
War Diary	Egypt.	15/03/1918	17/03/1918
War Diary	Tel-El-Kebir	15/03/1918	31/03/1918

WO 95/11586

4 CAV DIV TROOPS

COMBINED FIELD AMBULANCE

LUCKNOW

MHOW

SIALKOT

1917 JAN - 1918 APR

SIALKOT CAV FLD AMBULANCE

TO EGYPT 4 CAV DIV TROOPS

BEF
4 Cav Div.
Troops

Lucknow Cav Fld Amb

1917 Jan to 1918 Feb

To Egypt 4 Cav Div

SERIAL NO. 1774

Confidential

War Diary

of

LUCKNOW CAVALRY FIELD AMBULANCE. — 4th Cavalry Division

FROM 1st JANUARY 1917. TO 31st JANUARY 1917.

COMMITTEE FOR THE
MEDICAL HISTORY OF THE WAR
Date 23 APR. 1917

Army Form C. 2118.

WAR DIARY
or
INTELLIGENCE SUMMARY

(Erase heading not required.)

Instructions regarding War Diaries and Intelligence Summaries are contained in F.S. Regs., Part II. and the Staff Manual respectively. Title Pages will be prepared in manuscript.

Place	Date	Hour	Summary of Events and Information	Remarks and references to Appendices
ACHEUX	2/1/17		A course of instruction for the junior medical officers of the division was commenced. Some of the A.P.C. reported from Filgre Dubo at northern.	WHC
"	3/1/17		8 men of the A.P.C. reported from Filgre Dubo at northern. A scheme for the employment of the O.F.A. was in was submitted to higher authority today. The scheme is based on the principle that a O.F.A. should be a cavalry unit in fact that any movement of the O.F.A. involves the abandonment of the foundation of a man sharing station for in view of the immunity of the personnel of an adv. dressing station in the equipment being carried on pack animals. To carry it out the terms of ment of the F.S.T. with wagons would be used. In connection with the scheme a riding school for the A.F.C. has been started in this kind.	WHC WH Chisholm

2449 Wt. W14957/M90 750,000 1/16 J.B.C. & A. Forms/C.2118/12.

WAR DIARY or INTELLIGENCE SUMMARY

Army Form C. 2118.

Place	Date	Hour	Summary of Events and Information	Remarks and references to Appendices
ACHEUX	3/1/7		A message was received this (to me) a British medical officer to a place 10 or 12 miles away to see a British Officer who had met with an accident. The message came from the admins of the Div on the representations, I believe, of a General Officer. This incident indicates how handicapped the Service becomes by inadequate numbers of Indians with temp commissions in the place of British officers. The patients had already been seen by an Indian M.O. of the C.F.A. who was much nearer but had many British officers available to go. A British officer from these Indian M.S. officers available + go a British officer from there had to leave his work + travel in an ambulance car a distance of some 25 miles at great waste of time + petrol. Speaking generally, the Indian acting as an officer in the M.S. cannot replace a British M.O. in a F.D Amb. Such an officer has two separate + distinct functions (a) professional duties (b) routine military + discipline. Duties such as a regimental officer performs.	

W.H. Cayley

WAR DIARY
or
INTELLIGENCE SUMMARY

Army Form C.2118.

Place	Date	Hour	Summary of Events and Information	Remarks and references to Appendices
ACHEUX	3/1/17	(cont)	As regards the first (A) the Indian can only be used British Officers. British officers & also men often object to be treated by an Indian doctor. Moreover it has been my experience that even when an Indian M.S. Officer trains as regards his work must be supervised. (B) These Indian M.S. Officers have not got the necessary status nor authority (few of my dept nor, especially in a unit like this which has some 50 or 60 European troops in it. W.H. Anzag	
"	5/1/17		No T2/12635 D.H.W RUDD A.S.C M.T reprved the Dvnl from Dns S. Crws. Dept & was taken on the strength according. W.H.C	
"	12/1/17		No 367 2nd Cpl S/Sjy K.C. Vagheln was transferred to the Section. 905th Bn. C.F.A. & struck off the strength of this Unvnt. W.H.C	
"	15/1/17		One A.S.C. driver was was struck off strength of theny th W.H.C	

W.H.Anzag

Army Form C. 2118.

WAR DIARY
or
INTELLIGENCE SUMMARY
(Erase heading not required.)

Instructions regarding War Diaries and Intelligence Summaries are contained in F. S. Regs., Part II. and the Staff Manual respectively. Title Pages will be prepared in manuscript.

Place	Date	Hour	Summary of Events and Information	Remarks and references to Appendices
ACHEUX	23/1/17		Lieut. S.K. PHADKE I.M.S. (temp. 4 am.) Seconded CFA. 6th Cav Bde from was taken over the Shew field accordingly. Two horses (A.R.C.) were evacuated sick to Puchevis A.D.S.	
"	24/1/17		Lieut. D.C. CROLE R.A.M.C. left for duty with 1st Cav Div as attd Officer (A.H.C.) evacuated sick to h.h. C.C.S.	
"	30"		Lieut S.K. Phadke I.M.S.(T.C.) (received & attd) as Gen. officer. attd. Cav. Corp Anti-gas school.	
			Notes (1) During the entire part of the month very severe & cold has been experienced. The health of all ranks (including officers) has been good notwithstanding the cold. This members admitted into the Ambulance so far as Returns are concerned, have not increased. (2) Portable stretcher for use of evacuating our being constructed in this Unit.	W.H. Craig

"Medical"

Original

Confidential

War Diary

of

Lucknow Cav Field Ambulance

from 1.2.17 to 28.2.17

Medical

4th Cav. Division

Volume XXVII

Serial No. 177

COMMITTEE FOR THE
MEDICAL HISTORY OF THE WAR
Date 21 MAY 1917

Army Form C. 2118.

WAR DIARY
or
INTELLIGENCE SUMMARY
(Erase heading not required.)

Instructions regarding War Diaries and Intelligence Summaries are contained in F. S. Regs., Part II. and the Staff Manual respectively. Title Pages will be prepared in manuscript.

Place	Date	Hour	Summary of Events and Information	Remarks and references to Appendices
ACHEUX	2/2/17		One bearer (A.B.C.) evacuated sick & struck off strength	
"			One sweeper arrived. was taken on the strength	W.T.C
"	10/2/17		One bearer (A.B.C.) evacuated sick & struck off strength	W.T.C
"	11/2/17		One bearer (A.B.C.) evacuated sick & struck off strength	W.T.C
"	13/2/17		No latrines returned this regiment. Instructions received in this place have	
"	14/2/17		no riding horse received from Gn V.S. in place of one which died. There were	W.T.C
"	16/2/17		One St. A.S.C. H.T. evacuated sick & struck off strength. It was a case of	
"			mumps. All necessary precautions were taken.	
"			Three Prs. A.S.C. H.T. arrived to complete establishment. were taken on	
"	18/2/17		strength.	
"			One sweeper evacuated sick & struck off strength	W.T.C
"	26/2/17		During this month the Unit remained at ACHEUX, open for reception of sick	

W.H. Curgenl Maj
OC. E. Q.F.A.

2449 Wt. W14957/M90 750,000 1/16 J.B.C. & A. Forms/C.2118/12.

Confidential

War Diary

of

Lucknow. Cav. Field. Ambulance

from 1.3.17 to 31.3.17

Vol XXVIII

"Medical"
Original

COMMITTEE FOR THE
MEDICAL HISTORY OF THE WAR
Date —6 JUL. 1917

Army Form C. 2118.

WAR DIARY
or
INTELLIGENCE SUMMARY
(Erase heading not required.)

Instructions regarding War Diaries and Intelligence Summaries are contained in F. S. Regs., Part II. and the Staff Manual respectively. Title Pages will be prepared in manuscript.

Place	Hour	Summary of Events and Information	Remarks and references to Appendices
ACHEUX	2/1/17	One ASC HT Driver Returned from Conv. Depot. WTK	
"	12 3/17	Three A.M.C. men joined from Base WTK	
"	13 3/17	One man A.S.C. evacuated sick. One ASC HT Driver joined. One Mule died of ruptured diaphragm after being kicked by horse. Sgt. arrair. Sergt. HIRA SINGH left for a turn in LONDON WTK Two riding horses of Res. a Burns att 3 F. Amb sent to S.F. Car Dep WTK	
"	14 3/17	Orders received this morning (7.30 A.M.) for the unit to move with the 4th Cav. Bde to Fifth Army area. This CFA had a large hospital open for both British & Indian Patients had to be evacuated, every thing packed up & ACHEUX left before 11 A.M. of course this entails well to be done in the time last the Unit moved off at 3 P.m.	
MILLENCOURT	19 3/17	I think the question arises as to whether a Cav. F.A. should be asked to act as a sort of Stationary Hosp. considering how mobile any unit attached to Cavalry should be if it is to be efficient MILLENCOURT was reached about 9.30 P.M. in darkness & rain WTK Capt.	

2449 Wt. W14957/M90 750,000 1/16 J.B.C. & A. Forms/C.2118/12.

Army Form C. 2118.

WAR DIARY
or
INTELLIGENCE SUMMARY

(Erase heading not required.)

Instructions regarding War Diaries and Intelligence Summaries are contained in F. S. Regs., Part II. and the Staff Manual respectively. Title Pages will be prepared in manuscript.

Place	Hour	Summary of Events and Information	Remarks and references to Appendices
FRANQUEVILLE	20/3/17	Marched from MILLENCOURT at about 11 a.m. and arrived at [illegible] in FRANQUEVILLE in the afternoon about 3.30 p.m.	[illegible]
ALBERT-AVELUY Rd	21/3/17	Marched from FRANQUEVILLE at 10 a.m. The length of the march was about 30 miles. The length was difficult to for an Cav. Fd. Amb. to accompany Cavalry show that we marched so fast & not as Infantry. The limber wagons & light transport ambulances arrived at the place for Bivouac at with the officers & the few other mounted men at 9. p.m. Some of the mounted men on G.S. wagons arrived. With permission of the trans major, Albert, the unit billetted itself in some empty & ruined houses on the road leading to AVELUY which is about 1½ kilometres further on & in the neighbourhood of which most of the lt lt Cav Bde is bivouaced. The dismounted men arrived about 9 p.m. quite tired out. The ambs were too tired to allow of milk and care to return & pick them up.	WHC
"	22/3/17		

Army Form C. 2118.

WAR DIARY
or
INTELLIGENCE SUMMARY
(Erase heading not required.)

Instructions regarding War Diaries and Intelligence Summaries are contained in F.S. Regs., Part II. and the Staff Manual respectively. Title Pages will be prepared in manuscript.

Place	Hour	Summary of Events and Information	Remarks and references to Appendices
ALBERT-AVELUY Road 23/3/17		The G.S. waggons arrived this evening, extra teams having been sent back to fetch them in.	
" 28/3/17		Sub-Asst Surg: No 1311 JOYCE B.Q. was evacuated sick. WTC	
" 29/3/17		One native bearer of Rev A. Benn (Att. 2 k CFA) transferred to 4th Cav Bde WTC. One man A.B.C. evacuated sick. WTC	
" 30/3/17		One man A.S.C. M.T. evacuated sick. WTC. Sub Asst Surg: HIRA SINGH returned on return from his term of leave in England. He expressed in greatest appreciation of this privilege and everything connected with it. WTC	

W.T. C---
MAJOR I.M.S.
comdg. LUCKNOW CAV. FD. AMB.

"Medical"

Confidential

"Original"
April 1917

War Diary

of

Lucknow Cav Field Ambulance

from 1.4.17 to 30.4.17

Vol XXVIII

COMMITTEE FOR THE
MEDICAL HISTORY OF THE WAR
Date 6 JUL. 1917

Serial No. 444

Army Form C. 2118

WAR DIARY
or
INTELLIGENCE SUMMARY
(Erase heading not required.)

Place	Date	Hour	Summary of Events and Information	Remarks and references to Appendices
ALBERT - AVELUY RD	1/4/17		The following reinforcements received & taken on strength — one woman orderly one Bearer A.S.C. one sweeper	WTC
"	2/4/17		At 2.30 a.m. some 9 bombs dropped from German aeroplane fell in the vicinity of the billets. No casualties in this unit two among'st Horses remained quiet, attended by Stable piquet. Three men sleeping in a lister lorry close by were wounded & attended to by M.O. A.T.A. 1st Class H.S. Keeper CHANDAN LAL departed en route to leave. 1st Class H.S. Keeper NISSAR HUSSAIN who joined the unit from Indian Cav Base HQ. took over the duties from today.	WTC WTC
"	3/4/17		Two Bearers A.S.C. evacuated sick One Driver A.S.C. struck off strength. On Duties reports from hops & taken on strength.	WTC WTC
"	3/4/17		Two Sunbeam motor ambulance cars with their drivers exchanged for two Ford motor amb cars with their drivers	WTC

W.H.Coy.

Army Form C. 2118

WAR DIARY
or
INTELLIGENCE SUMMARY
(Erase heading not required.)

Instructions regarding War Diaries and Intelligence Summaries are contained in F. S. Regs., Part II. and the Staff Manual respectively. Title Pages will be prepared in manuscript.

Place	Date	Hour	Summary of Events and Information	Remarks and references to Appendices
IRLES	8/4/17		This unit with 4th Cav Div, marched at 8 a.m. to IRLES (Cavalry) in a field at side of road between MIRAMONT & IRLES. Weather bright but very cold. WTC	
IRLES	9/4/17		Weather today very inclement with severe winter weather much snow. At 5 p.m. unit held in readiness to move. One pack stove Griffiths evacuated sick. WTC	
IRLES	10/4/17		'A' echelon marched at 2.30 a.m., arrived at SAPIGNIES at 7.30 a.m. & received orders immediately to return to former camp, which was reached at 11 a.m. Weather exceedingly severe, lately cold wind & heavy snow. WTC	
IRLES	11/4/17		'A' echelon marched at 6 a.m. beyond SAPIGNIES through ERVILLERS to and remained on side of ERVILLERS - MORY Rd. Came under slight hostile shell fire. Pack mounted section attached to Lucknow Bde. A med. Officer sent to a main Dressing Station at MORY & dealt with Indian wounded. Remen Division tied rec'd to horsey Lucknow Bde. was not engaged & unit marched back to IRLES at 6.30 pm. arriving midnight in a snow blizzard. Men thrown about down up, motorcycle broken & came out of action. WTC Cropley	

WAR DIARY
or
INTELLIGENCE SUMMARY

Army Form C. 2118

Place	Date	Hour	Summary of Events and Information	Remarks and references to Appendices
IRLES	12/4/17		Remained in camp. Weather most inclement - cold, wet & snowing at times. New 4 animals rested. Crew repaired tents, motors, they likewise went over broken ups & two not yet been repaired. No rations for men or animals so iron rations consumed. Dinners under 2 hrs notice to move. WPC	
AVELUY	13/4/17		Weather still wet but fair & fine. Marched with Lucknow Cav. Bde to AVELUY where unit was billetted in huts. No shells for horses.	
BUS-LES-ARTOIS	14/4/17		Unit marched at 11 A.M. with Lucknow Cav Bde to BUS-LES-ARTOIS arrived 3 P.M. Men billetted in huts. Shelter for almost half the animals in horse standings. Weather fine & warmer. WPC	
"	15/4/17		Resting with pain - CW. WPC	
"	16/4/17		The Supply Sergeant A.S.C. having been reverted to his permanent rank of Corporal for an offence, became surplus to establishment & is struck off the strength & returned to Base accordingly. WPC Three Bearers A.B.I. evacuated sick & struck off strength. WPC	
"	19/4/17		Two motor bicycles having broken down, were returned to Workshops & struck off strength from A.F. B.13½. One motor bicycle was received on 16th April and taken on strength. RHCanf	

1875 Wt. W593/826 1,000,000 4/15 J.B.C. & A. A.D.S.S./Forms/C. 2118.

WAR DIARY
or
INTELLIGENCE SUMMARY

(Erase heading not required.)

Army Form C. 2118

Instructions regarding War Diaries and Intelligence Summaries are contained in F. S. Regs., Part II. and the Staff Manual respectively. Title Pages will be prepared in manuscript.

Place	Date	Hour	Summary of Events and Information	Remarks and references to Appendices
BUS-LES-ARTOIS	22/4/17		One motor lorry etc received & taken on strength WHC	
"	28/4/17		One horses etc. evacuated sick & struck off strength WHC	
"	29/4/17		Four drivers also joined from Base and taken on the strength WHC	
"	30/4/17		Unit still camped in tents at BUS-LES-ARTOIS and hospital open for reception of sick of the Northern Corr. Base &c. WHC Anzy	

Confidential

War Diary

of

Lucknow Cavalry Field Ambulance

from 1.5.17 to 31.5.17

Vol XXIX

"medical"

Serial No. 124

From 1st May to 30th June 1917

COMMITTEE FOR THE MEDICAL HISTORY OF THE WAR
Date 27 JUL. 1917

Army Form C. 2118

WAR DIARY
or
INTELLIGENCE SUMMARY
(Erase heading not required.)

Instructions regarding War Diaries and Intelligence Summaries are contained in F.S. Regs., Part II. and the Staff Manual respectively. Title Pages will be prepared in manuscript.

Place	Date	Hour	Summary of Events and Information	Remarks and references to Appendices
BUS-LES-ARTOIS	May 1st		In camp in temporary huts with a hospital tpen for sick of Lucknow Cav Bde & local sick	WTC
"	2nd		Sgt. acrot Sgt. Joyce returned here from on discharge from hospital	WTC
"	3rd		Lieut. Rockwin Wd. & 13 O.R. (proceeded) to No 3 Canadian Stationary Hosp. for temporary duty.	WTC
			The above party returned to unit.	WTC
"	10th		One Duff & two & no mans A.B.C. (reserve) as rein forcements & taken on the strength	WTC
"	13th		The Sergeant major and one sweeper evacuated sick.	WTC
"	14th		The Lucknow C.F.A. marched at 6 a.m. with the Lucknow Cav Bde on moving of the 4th Cav Div. Arrived at bivouacs at MEAULT at 11 a.m.	WTC
MEAULT	15th			

1875 Wt. W593/826 1,000,000 4/15 J.B.C. & A. A.D.S.S./Forms/C. 2118.

Army Form C. 2118

WAR DIARY
or
INTELLIGENCE SUMMARY
(Erase heading not required.)

Instructions regarding War Diaries and Intelligence Summaries are contained in F.S. Regs., Part II. and the Staff Manual respectively. Title Pages will be prepared in manuscript.

Place	Date	Hour	Summary of Events and Information	Remarks and references to Appendices
SUZANNE	16/5/17		Marched from MEAULT at 6.45 am, and arrived at Suzanne in SUZANNE at 10.30 am. Weather cold & wet.	WHC
St CREN	17/5/17 18/5/17		Marched from SUZANNE at 9.15 am, arrived at St CREN 5.30 pm. Went into bivouac in the fields at St CREN this unit continues with Sec C.F.A. under command of Lt Col Fleming M.S. to form a main dressing station in huts & tents. The Sec C.F.A. along had an advanced dressing station at JEANCOURT. The main Dressing Station receives patients from 4th & 5th Cav Div & from 5th C. Div.	WHC WHC
"	19/5/17		One Driver A.S.C. (M.T.) evacuated sick. One sweeper received. No reinforcement taken in strength.	WHC

(Sd) Cooper

Army Form C. 2118

WAR DIARY
or
INTELLIGENCE SUMMARY
(Erase heading not required.)

Instructions regarding War Diaries and Intelligence Summaries are contained in F. S. Regs., Part II. and the Staff Manual respectively. Title Pages will be prepared in manuscript.

Place	Date	Hour	Summary of Events and Information	Remarks and references to Appendices
ST CREN	30/5/17		Under F.S. Reg. Part II Chapter XVI paras 129.1. and para 140.5.x I offer the following remarks for consideration. The office work required of a Divl. F.I. Amb. is so great that the forms from quite above would not appear to leave (stop) the text of War. Every day seven daily states have to be prepared and submitted & a lot of extra information added. There are about 15 weekly returns & 20 monthly returns, most of them having to be submitted on manuscript forms as ruled out & written every time. Over a thousand separate memos & letters are written during the year. Special reports involving much time & trouble in preparation are often called for. At a time when the Ambulance is busiest i.e. when dealing with wounded special casualty lists have daily to be sent & extra a prompt report has to be written whenever a group of casualties are admitted, giving not only particulars of the cases but the location of the engagement & an account of the circumstances in which the casualties were brought in. W.Popp	

1875 Wt. W593/826 1,000,000 4/15 J.B.C. & A. A.D.S.S./Forms/C. 2118.

Army Form C. 2118

WAR DIARY
or
INTELLIGENCE SUMMARY
(Erase heading not required.)

Instructions regarding War Diaries and Intelligence Summaries are contained in F. S. Regs., Part II. and the Staff Manual respectively. Title Pages will be prepared in manuscript.

Place	Date	Hour	Summary of Events and Information	Remarks and references to Appendices
St CREN	30/5/17 (cont)		In addition the office work involved in feeding, clothing, paying & maintaining discipline in the unit has to be done & numerous others form of office work. Owing to War Establishment Pt XVII it will be found that not a single clerk is allowed for a Cav Fd Amb of an Indian Cav Div in France. What staff then is available for all this office work? It cannot be done by ward orderlies, Army Bearer Corps or menial followers attached transport personnel. The only people to do it are the officers, the two SNCO assistant surgeons, the pack store Sergt, not the few British nursing orderlies (two in W.E. Pt XVII actually 5 in this unit). The first need not be exhausted. It is obvious that if employed one or more of the SNCOs Assist Surgs & British nursing orderlies are employed in the offices, (as they are + must be) the treatment & nursing of the sick & wounded must suffer. WM Cap...	

Confidential

War Diary

of

Lucknow C.F.A

from 1.6.17 to 30.6.17

Vol XXIX

WAR DIARY or INTELLIGENCE SUMMARY

Army Form C. 2118

Place	Date	Hour	Summary of Events and Information	Remarks and references to Appendices
ST CREN	1/6/19		The advance CFA is at St Oren, closed out leaving its personnel to the Secunderabad CFA to form a main Dressing Station receiving sick and wounded from the H.Q. & 3rd Cav Div, SG 1 Div & other troops. No 16940 a/Sergt Major MUSGRAVE P.H. RAMC. having been discharged to duty from No 3 Can 87h Hosp, returned the unit for duty.	WTC
	2/6/19		Secunderabad CFA left ST CREN and those last opened a Regt Station for both British and Indian troops of the 4th & 5th Cav Brig and other troops in the neighbourhood. The accommodation for this work is good. There is a large farm house, with its out buildings all in a fairly good state of repair. Also eleven marquee tents and a French hut holding 30 patients. Also two marquees and one bell tent. 30 British and 28 Indian patients were taken over from Sec CFA. Capt G.A. Romney CAMC & 9 O.R. Canadians joined for temporary duty. This personnel belongs to No 7 Canadian CFA.	WTC Capt

WAR DIARY
or
INTELLIGENCE SUMMARY

Army Form C. 2118

(Erase heading not required.)

Place	Date	Hour	Summary of Events and Information	Remarks and references to Appendices
ST. OMER	3/6/17		Two Drivers A.S.C. M.T. arrived were taken on the Strength. W.M.C.	
"	10/6/17		Capt. G.A. Ramsay C.A.M.C. this Afternoon left & reported their Unit W.M.C.	
"	15/6/17		10 O.R.C. men detached for temporary duty Ambulance C.F.A. at then advanced Dressing Station. W.M.C.	
"	17/6/17		The weather has been hot & fine during the past fortnight. W.M.C.	
"	26/6/17		The weather since last entry has been rather with thunderstorms and rain. W.M.C.	
"	30/6/17		Major F.W.E. Coghlin I.M.S. proceeded on leave to U.K.— yesterday 29th inst. Capt. F.W. Campbell R.Mac. proceeded on 14 days leave to U.K. to-day 30th. & Captain W. Griffiths from the same took over temporary command. 10.?MB	

W McC. Capt.
Name

Confidential

War Diary

of

Lucknow C.F.A

from 1.7.17 to 31.7.17

Vol XXX

"Medical"
Original

Serial No. 144

WAR DIARY
or
INTELLIGENCE SUMMARY

(Erase heading not required.)

Army Form C. 2118

Place	Date	Hour	Summary of Events and Information	Remarks and references to Appendices
S. Creu	1/7/17		A Party confined in under left. The morning to report to his O/C Jackson C.T.A. for Learners duty - No Employers bearer Party. 1 Sub west Serveyor. 3 British O.R. WJ 31 Army horses Corps. WJ The above party reported his unit this morning. WJ	
do	3/7/17		The Undermentioned party proceeded this day to DOINGT to assist in hay making, one farm horse - Three G.S. Wagons complete with Eight L.D. horses and four L.D. horses - Spare. WJ Twelve A.S.C. (H.T.) men - Twenty Eight A.B.C. men WJ -	
do	8/7/17			
do	9/7/17		Weather hot three days. Showery with Thunder. WJ - W. Jones	

Army Form C. 2118

WAR DIARY
or
INTELLIGENCE SUMMARY
(Erase heading not required.)

Instructions regarding War Diaries and Intelligence Summaries are contained in F.S. Regs., Part II. and the Staff Manual respectively. Title Pages will be prepared in manuscript.

Place	Date	Hour	Summary of Events and Information	Remarks and references to Appendices
ST OMER	9/7/17		Major W.H. CAZALY RMS rejoined this morning having returned from 10 days leave to England. Six riding horses, being surplus to the Est. laid down in W.E. Paw XVIII, were this morning sent to Re. 1. K.D.G's and Stowle off the strength of this Unit, according to orders of M.G.C. 2nd Dir. For the last two years or more a mounted party of M.L.S. sometimes being 10 mounted orderlies, sometimes + known as the "Pack Grenade" Section" have been opposed in this Unit & render first aid to Casualty in action when wheels are unable to accompany the troops & Bearers on foot are unable to keep up. This mounted party requires a minimum of 11 riding horses & 2 pack animals. With the loss of the above 6 horses the Pack M'd also 6 other units either be abolished on its what if to continue hunts of the Unit. (Including the C.O. & Transport horses). Total W.E.P. XVII allows only 4 horses + 7 ponies for the whole ambulance.	

(Sd) W.H. Cazaly

WAR DIARY
or
INTELLIGENCE SUMMARY

(Erase heading not required.)

Army Form C. 2118

Place	Date	Hour	Summary of Events and Information	Remarks and references to Appendices
ST CREN	12/1/19		Capt Ramsay C.A.M.C. with two Batmen and 8 O.R.s from No 7 Can stat. can Fd Amb. (who have been attached to this Unit for temporary duty) returned to their own Unit this morning. With reference to this temporary addition to the staff I think a few remarks as to the War establishment of this Unit may be useful for future reference. The amount of office work in a F.D. Amb. is very great considering what a small unit it is. Not only have reports & returns to connection with the patients (the admittries & forms & returns clothing, medicines to be for patients to the armies) for but there is the ordinary routine orderly room work to be done for the personnel. This includes (of others & carrying on) clothing pay, Burials etc, & the draughty of orders & carrying on of the same for as in a regiment. No provision is made for orderly room clerks. It is true that R.S.O. a month is allowed for three writers but this does not provide the writers. W.T. Craig	

WAR DIARY
or
INTELLIGENCE SUMMARY
(Erase heading not required.)

Army Form C. 2118

Place | **Date** | **Hour** | **Summary of Events and Information** | **Remarks and references to Appendices**

Unemployed Sub Asst Surgeons & British nursing orderlies, of whom there are very few, have to be taken from their legitimate work and employed in the office, and the more patients dealt with the fewer the number of those available for work & therefore the lower the Sanitary & orderlies can give to the patients. The inference is obvious. There are other defects in the establishment of which perhaps the most most felt is the absence of a Quartermaster Sergeant. To do this work of such a man there is only the store keeper & he is in a different unit which he is not very often in my experience to have charge & do to look after the returns & the patients & has been found necessary to make the Pack Store Sergeant act as Q.M. Sergt. & his time is fully occupied with this work, which involves all the supplies & introduces a number of patients until. So that when there are as at all a number of patients nursing orderlies have to be detached to work in the Pack Store. Again the question of attending to the patients, the actual work of the nursing orderlies, arises.

W.T. Craig?

WAR DIARY
or
INTELLIGENCE SUMMARY
(Erase heading not required.)

Army Form C. 2118

Instructions regarding War Diaries and Intelligence Summaries are contained in F.S. Regs., Part II. and the Staff Manual respectively. Title Pages will be prepared in manuscript.

Place	Date	Hour	Summary of Events and Information	Remarks and references to Appendices
			Again, to run a J.D. Amb. efficiently it is necessary to have certain skilled workmen such as carpenters, those workmen & trailers are not provided. It is true that Rs/- a month is allowed for their carpenters but unless there happens to be a carpenter in the Regt, which there is not, the allowance does not provide them, any if there was such workmen they have to be taken from their legitimate work & they would annoy the few British personnel we would be most unfortunate to have of them. The provision of lights too, is inadequate. These are from butter followers enlarged no lamps of these are one for British ranks. They are very bad at cooking European food & one careless as cooks for Indians on account of their caste. If we have two extra ones i.e. for Hindoos & one for Mahomedans This is not nearly enough & also renders it impossible to provide a decent for detached parties. I am strongly of opinion that, in the light of the experience gained during the past war, the war establishment regime immediate revision. W.H. Bagg	

Army Form C. 2118.

WAR DIARY
or
INTELLIGENCE SUMMARY

(Erase heading not required.)

Instructions regarding War Diaries and Intelligence Summaries are contained in F. S. Regs., Part II and the Staff Manual respectively. Title Pages will be prepared in manuscript.

Place	Date	Hour	Summary of Events and Information	Remarks and references to Appendices
St. CREN	13/7/17		One wed rating detached for temp: duty in a troop! for labour company.	
"	15/7/17		Three L.D. Horses received from Base & taken on strength to complete establishment.	
"	23/7/17		Lieut. P. F. Larkin has returned for temp: duty with a working party at VENDELLES. This with Capt Campbell away since June 29th & not likely to return, and Lieut. Plunkett on leave & Lieut Dickson detached there are only two officers left to carry on the work of this Unit. WTC a request for another extra return containing information which could be got from AF B213 suggests that arrears retention is not (gain) to F.S. Regs! Part II Chap XVI Sect. 129 Para 1.	
"	26/7/17			
"	31/7/17		The work of the Unit during this month has been chiefly that of acting as a Div. Rem. Station, receiving & returning to duty in many slight cases, as previous. The weather on the whole has been fine & warmer though somewhat wetter than last month.	

W.T. Crisp
Major (?) Ind.
O.C. L. CFAH.

Confidential

WAR DIARY
of
Lucknow Cavalry Field Ambulance

from 1.8.17 to 31.8.17

Vol XXXI

Original
"medical"

COMMITTEE FOR THE
MEDICAL HISTORY OF THE WAR
Date 16 OCT 1917

Serial No: 144

Army Form C. 2118.

WAR DIARY
or
INTELLIGENCE SUMMARY

(Erase heading not required.)

Instructions regarding War Diaries and Intelligence Summaries are contained in F.S. Regs, Part II. and the Staff Manual respectively. Title Pages will be prepared in manuscript.

Place	Date	Hour	Summary of Events and Information	Remarks and references to Appendices
ST CREN	1/8/17		The Lucknow C.F.A. is still open at ST CREN, acting as a Hospital for Slight cases, i.e. as a Div Rest Station, in addition to whatever patients arrive from the neighbourhood.	
"	4/8/17		Capt F.W. Campbell R.A.M.C. T.O., struck off the strength of the Unit from July 14th 1917 in accordance with W.D. Telegram no 24/C/256 (A.M.D.) of 29.7.17 & communicated ??? form ???9y.	W.T.C
"	5/8/17		1st Lieutenant E.T. WYMAN Medical Reserve Corps Enlisted States Army reported his arrival today from 4: Can Div Reserve Park and was taken on the strength of the Lucknow C.F.A. vice Capt. F.W. Campbell R.A.M.C. The Lucknow C.F.A. left ST CREN this morning, after handing over the Hospital and Rest Station to Sialkot C.F.A., together with much ampho & Red Cross equipment.	W.T.C.
ST CHRIST	6/8/17		A party of 2 officers, 10 British other ranks & 443 Indians (including horse transport and two motor amb cars) with the necessary equipment was despatched to VILLERS FAUCON and EPÉHY to form first & main & advanced dressing station under the orders of the A.D.M.S. 33.rd Div. for the treatment of sickness of the 4th Cav. Dismounted Brigade which took over part of the front line to day. The dressing stations are under the orders of the O.C.'s 107 & 106 F.D. R.amb's. The remainder of the Unit went into Bivouacs (tents & temp shelters) near ST CHRIST near this Camp to form a Hospital. There is no accommodation in this Camp to form a Hospital.	W.T.C Capt

WAR DIARY
INTELLIGENCE SUMMARY
(Erase heading not required.)

Army Form C. 2118.

Place	Date	Hour	Summary of Events and Information	Remarks and references to Appendices
St CHRIST	7/8/17		An A.S.C. Supply Sergeant arrived to complete establishment and was taken on the strength.	WTTC
"	8/8/17		A hosp. Stove keeper returned to same as complete to establishment, having been replaced by another who arrived 5/5/17.	KTTC
"	20/8/17		Lieut P.F. Larkwi I.M.S, T.O. deputed for duty with the VI Corps and is struck off the strength of the Unit accordingly.	WTTC
"	22/8/17		Four nurses A.B.C. arrived from the Base as reinforcements and were taken on the strength accordingly.	WTTC
"	24/8/17		No. LHR/1639 2nd Grade Hospital Store keeper MOHAMED SHARIF 9+T Corps having been granted leave yesterday from 7 a.m. to 9 p.m. for the purpose of going to Amiens, failed to return from leave. His A.P.M. 4th Army Div. so absent without leave. True des criptors furnished.	WTC
"	25/8/17		H S K Mohamed Sharif notified to A.P.M. 4th Army Div as absent without leave. True descriptors furnished.	WTC
"	27/8/17		Capt F.W. RIGBY R.A.M.C. (T.C.) reports his arrival for duty and is taken on the strength accordingly.	WTC
St CHRIST	31/8/17		2. E.F.A. still remains as during the month	WT

W.T. Craig

Original "medical" Adrian

Confidential

War Diary

of

LUCKNOW CAV FD. AMB.

from 1.9.17 to 30.9.17

Vol XXXII

COMMITTEE FOR THE MEDICAL HISTORY OF THE WAR
Date 12 DEC. 1917

Serial No. 144

Army Form C. 2118.

WAR DIARY
or
INTELLIGENCE SUMMARY

(Erase heading not required.)

Instructions regarding War Diaries and Intelligence Summaries are contained in F. S. Regs., Part II. and the Staff Manual respectively. Title Pages will be prepared in manuscript.

Place	Date	Hour	Summary of Events and Information	Remarks and references to Appendices
St CHRIST	1/9/17		The Lucknow C.F.A. remains as before, at ST CHRIST is the head 9ptrs with an open dispensary but no hospital. At VADENCOURT is a Bn forming attached to the advanced Dressing station of No 104 Fd. Amb. Consists of one officer, 4 British & about 24 Indian O.R.s. At PŒUILLY at HQ of No 104 Fd. Amb is one officer I/c of a small party from Another C.F.A. At JEANCOURT is one Sub.-advnt Surgeon and 6 Indian O.R.s attached to the advd. Dr. Station of No 102 Fd. Amb.	WTHC
"	2/9/17		One cook A.H.C. & one British O. & T. evacuated sick	WTHC
"	3/9/17		One cook Att.C. evacuated sick. This leaves no cooks at all for British patients	WTHC
"	4/9/17		A bearer of the A.B.C. tried by S.C.M. & sentenced to 30 lashes.	WTHC
"	5/9/17		The punishment of yesterday's S.C.M. was inflicted on prisoners today.	WTHC
"	6/9/17		A clear field to myself to instructions in the use of the new Fd. Med. Card & to submit to D.H.Q. a letter pointing out defects in the and 1 suggesting improvements. esp to be written & exemplifying casualties with sick & wounded.	WTHC

WAR DIARY
or
INTELLIGENCE SUMMARY
(Erase heading not required.)

Army Form C.2118.

Place	Date	Hour	Summary of Events and Information	Remarks and references to Appendices
St CHRIST	10/9/17		One Sweeper S+T O. evacuated sick MTC	
"	13/9/17		One Bearer A.P.C. taken on strength on his transfer to this unit from Amb H.Q. WTFC	
"	17/9/17		One Bhisty A.H.C. taken on strength. WTFC	
"	18/9/17		One Cook (3/1 T.C.) joined & was taken on the strength. This is a boy about 15 years of age, who was a "tennis chicken" before enlistment & states he was enlisted as a "tennis chicken". He seems nothing whatever of cookery for British patients & is therefore useless. The facts have been reported to D.A.Q. The unit. cannot deal with British patients without cooks competent to cook for them. WTFC	
"	20/9/17		One Cook S+T evacuated sick LATE	
"	21/9/17		The S+T cook referred to in note of 18" returned to Amb. Ct.A. and another cook A.H.C. to join from that unit. WTFC	
"	22/9/17		One R D Nurse enlist for "old age & wornout" & one made for crèche. Both struck off strength. Total 4. WTFC	
"	23/9/17		Lieut. S. K. PHADKE I.M.S.(T.C.) transferred to 36 I. Nurse and struck off strength of unit WTFC	

Army Form C. 2118.

WAR DIARY
or
INTELLIGENCE SUMMARY

(Erase heading not required.)

Instructions regarding War Diaries and Intelligence Summaries are contained in F. S. Regs., Part II. and the Staff Manual respectively. Title Pages will be prepared in manuscript.

Place	Date	Hour	Summary of Events and Information	Remarks and references to Appendices
St CHRIST	24 9/17		The Senior O.P.C. transferred to Comd. O.F.A. & struck off strength WMTC. Lieut A.R. GEYER RAMC (T.C.) reported his arrival for duty with the unit. Two taken on the strength	WMTC
"	25 9/17		On T.S. from Dr E. Reynolds A.S.C. att 2/1th L.C.F.A. recaptured two escaped German prisoners.	WMTC
"	26 9/17		One P.o. a3c MT motor cyclist transferred to Rouen & struck off the strength.	WMTC
	29 9/17		One Pte a3c MT reported his arrival as motor cyclist from 1st base WMTC on the strength	WMTC
	30 9/17		A Hosp Store Keeper pmnt class taken on the strength of the unit vice a deserter. The weather during the latter half of September has been exceptionally fine throughout.	WMTC

W.H.Geyer

Confidential

WAR DIARY

of

Lucknow Cav Fd Ambulance

from 1.10.17 to 31.10.17

Vol XXXIII

WAR DIARY
or
INTELLIGENCE SUMMARY

Army Form C. 2118.

Place	Date	Hour	Summary of Events and Information	Remarks and references to Appendices
ST CHRIST	1/X/17		The 2 C.F.A. is still in camp near the ruined village of ST CHRIST. In hospital is Major as there is no accommodation for sick. All patients are at once transferred to 5th Divl: C.F.A. elsewhere. The parties forming the advanced dumping stations in the front line returned & reported the dump taken over by us it. Our division taken out of the line. W.T.F.C.	
"	3/X/17		One wound only. Movements such & struck off the strength. W.T.F.C.	
"	4/X/17		Lieut A.K. MENON M.B.S. (T.C.) joined the 2 C.F.A. for duty. This officer is a native of the Malabar coast India and cannot speak Hindustani or any other language spoken by the Indian troops nor during his tour of military training this sphere of usefulness has a T.C. appt. is very limited.	W.T.F.C.
"	6/X/17		Capt F.W. RIGBY R.AM.C. (T.C.) was transferred to 24" Div & left the 2 C.F.A. today.	W.T.F.C.
"	7/X/17		One Cmbr A.H.C. joined for duty, 3 ORs taken on the strength. 107 T.C. The weather during the last three days has completely changed from warm fine sunny days to wet cold stormy weather. The animals are out in the open, the officers men occupying tents or improvised bivouacs. W.T.F.C. Angus	

Army Form C. 2118.

WAR DIARY
or
INTELLIGENCE SUMMARY
(Erase heading not required.)

Instructions regarding War Diaries and Intelligence Summaries are contained in F. S. Regs., Part II. and the Staff Manual respectively. Title Pages will be prepared in manuscript.

Place	Date	Hour	Summary of Events and Information	Remarks and references to Appendices
St CHARLES	10/10/17		Major Last Cagely I.M.S. proceeded on leave from his unit to join his unit to the United Kingdom	
	11/10/17		Capt R.F. Jones, taken over command of unit on Major Cagely's departure M.O.	
	13/10/17		One L.B. House was on L.D. and arranged for permanent night duty & later in the hospital.	
"	18/10/17		Major Cagely's leave has been extended to the 9th Apl	
"	19/10/17		On return having been evacuated sick to Hospital in strength of his unit NCO.	
	19/10/17		A Medical Review was held yesterday. Answer & P.M. Evolution & have went Pathanpolian refs.	
"	19/10/17		Hospital JR/Mess M.A.M.B.D. SHARIEF, N.T.C. was appointed by the Military Police in AMIENS & brought to his new residence by W.F.Ross Capt RAMC	

Army Form C. 2118.

WAR DIARY
or
INTELLIGENCE SUMMARY

(Erase heading not required.)

Instructions regarding War Diaries and Intelligence Summaries are contained in F. S. Regs., Part II. and the Staff Manual respectively. Title Pages will be prepared in manuscript.

Place	Date	Hour	Summary of Events and Information	Remarks and references to Appendices
SE CHRIST	22/9/17	-	One Sergeant S + T.C. + one Cpl. S + T.C. Orderlies arrived from E.E.F. Base Depot + taken on strength. WJ	
"	23/9/17		One Driver A.S.C. M.T. having been evacuated sick to hospital is struck off strength. WJ	
"	28/9/17		One Driver A.S.C. M.T. having joined the R.F.C. in service previous to his 13th September has been struck off strength. WJ Weather extremely unsettled, windy and showery. WJ	
"	30/9/17			
"	30/9/17		A summary General Court Martial assembled to enquire into the case of H.S.S.K. MOHAMED SHARIF and charged Desertion. WJ Major Donald Cave Camp 72 Lieutenants CDO	

Confidential

War Diary

of

LUCKNOW
CAVALRY FIELD AMBULANCE.

from 1.11.17 to 30.11.17

Vol XXXIV

Army Form C. 2118.

WAR DIARY
or
INTELLIGENCE SUMMARY.
(Erase heading not required.)

Instructions regarding War Diaries and Intelligence Summaries are contained in F.S. Regs., Part II. and the Staff Manual respectively. Title pages will be prepared in manuscript.

Place	Date	Hour	Summary of Events and Information	Remarks and references to Appendices
St Christ	3/11/17	—	Orderly duties mostly from Indian General Base depot MARSEILLES, for duty with this unit WGJ	
"	4/11/17		Br Cpl R.S. + T.C. reported sick WGJ	
"	5/11/17		Pte P.E. RAME (pnr) he was on a clerk shop RAC HT duties gives to duty with his unit WGJ	
"	7/11/17		Pte insp S. + T.C. having been vaccinated dies of BRMC 11 hr therapy of he went from his St unit WGJ	
"	7/11/17		H.S.K. MOHAMED SHARIFF two orderlies of S.B.O.M. L duen (?) Iwno ih a probation & trump of deserting the duties was promulgated a parade this day WGJ he was dump + WGJ allowing will remain WGJ	
"	8/11/17		Captain W.G. Jones, R.A.M.C. proceeded on 14 days leave to the United Kingdom A Geyer RR RAMC	

WAR DIARY
or
INTELLIGENCE SUMMARY.
(Erase heading not required.)

Army Form C. 2118.

Place	Date	Hour	Summary of Events and Information	Remarks and references to Appendices
At Chapois	9/11/17		Lieut. A.E.K. Menon J.M.S (T.C.) transferred to No 68 Labour Group, this day	
At Chapois	9/11/17		Lieut. S.M. Sahyal J.M.S (T.C.) formed the unit from 68 L Labour Group.	
St CHRIST	10/11/17		Major W.H. CAZALY M.S. having returned the Unit from Officers, 30 days leave to the U.K. returned. transferred	
"	11.11.17		Inspected A GOGUET CHAPOIS with this horse was transferred from HQ 4 Cav Divn	M.T.O.
"	12.11.17		One man A.S.C.M.T. evacuated sick & struck off the strength to midnight. The A.S.C. 4th Division (one) from 4th Cav Bde Reserve Park and three drivers (of the unit temporarily) on duty to 4th M.C. was inspected	4/11/c
"	13.11.17		This afternoon the "Pack transport Section" paraded fully equipped. The section of the LUCKNOW CFA consists of two Officers and addition. all mounted and with two pack animals in addition. It is found on the authority of the 4th Div. 3 Cav Corps	
			9 O.R's	

WAR DIARY or INTELLIGENCE SUMMARY

Army Form C. 2118.

Place	Date	Hour	Summary of Events and Information	Remarks and references to Appendices
(continued)			However useful this branch of the CFA may be, the fact remains that it is not officiered [officered] properly in any of the troops and that war conditions makes no provision for it. Consequently its formation involves the dismounting of all mounted ranks except the Officers & Transport Sergeant, including such people as the Sqn. Sgt. Majors, R.Q.M.S. B echelon & both subordinate employers. It seems impossible to use up of all the spare transport animals. This seems but at a time when the unit is put into action and its most strenuous extra use maybe can, it its mobility would be seriously impaired by having a large number of army its animals or even the remainder of reductions in even more abnormal conditions. Therefore, before so seriously impairing the efficiency of the CFA a while I venture to think it would be better to obtain sanction for the necessary extra horses (12 Cleves) before actually forming the "Pack mounts" section in action. W.H. Cay[?]	

WAR DIARY
INTELLIGENCE SUMMARY

Army Form C. 2118.

Place	Date	Hour	Summary of Events and Information	Remarks and references to Appendices
ST CHRIST	16/1/17		The team of A.S.C. M.T. & the both A.H.C. surrendered Rifle	W.H.C.
"	18/1/17		The men of the MT Pool the Unit	W.H.C.
LONGAVESNE	19/1/17		'A' Echelon & the L.C.F.A. marched at 3 p.m. at LONGAVESNE with the Luckrow Cav. Bde in anticipation of active operations against the enemy.	
"	20/1/17		At 6.30 a.m. this morning the Luckrow Cav. Bde moved forward and at night reached a point near les VACQUERIE which had been occupied by the enemy in the morning. The O.C. L.C.F.A. accompanied Bde HQ & the Pack horses Sect went with the Bde. The Shortage of riding animals in the Unit was acutely felt. The P.M.S. could only be organised by using all the spare Transport animals, and dismount the S.A. Surgeons, Sup, Majors & Others. No horse, except to change, is of an Officer on leave, was available to carry the C.O.'s orderly. This Shortage of animals is a serious menace to the efficiency of the Unit. 24 horses & 3 horse ambulances also started with the Bde but only the 'A' Echelon remained at LONGAVESNE. The Bde A ccte and the L.C.F.A. LONGAVESNE is between the Bde A ccte and the L.C.F.A.	W.H. Coury

Army Form C. 2118.

WAR DIARY
or
INTELLIGENCE SUMMARY.
(Erase heading not required.)

Place	Date	Hour	Summary of Events and Information	Remarks and references to Appendices
FINS	21/11/17		The Brabazon Cav Bde remained near the place where the night was spent until about 5 p.m. when it marched to FINS. The 1. C.F.A. (2nd C.O. & P.M.S.) left LONGAVESNE and advanced to a point 2 miles N of GOUZEAUCOURT & spent night there	W.H.C.
"	22/11/17		Remained at FINS where the whole C.F.A. including B echelon assembled together again.	W.H.C.
FOURQUES	23/11/17		At 12 noon the whole 1. C.F.A. marched to FOURQUES to the billets & bivouacs formerly occupied by the Ambulance C.F.A.	W.H.C.
"	24/11/17	8. a.m.	The whole 4th Can Div & hnqrs 1. C.F.A. (plus in) no one turns notice to move.	W.H.C.
"	25/11/17	5.30 a.m.	B echelon marched to VILLERS-FAUCON, arriving about 10.30 a.m. The C.O. & P.M.S. joined the Ancheux Cav Bde. This time the P.M.S. was 3 short, 2 animals being sick & one reporting for C.D.S. orders. 3. p.m. The Div returned to ATHIES area, the 1. C.F.A. returning to FOURQUES. The dismounted men were brought back in lorries. One man of ASC M.T. proceed to Trinité.	W.H. Cargy

Army Form C. 2118.

WAR DIARY
or
INTELLIGENCE SUMMARY.
(Erase heading not required.)

Instructions regarding War Diaries and Intelligence Summaries are contained in F. S. Regs., Part II. and the Staff Manual respectively. Title pages will be prepared in manuscript.

Place	Date	Hour	Summary of Events and Information	Remarks and references to Appendices
FOURQUES	27/11/17		One man of the ASC HT & one Syce S & T Corps evacuated sick	W.T.C. MTC
"	28/11/17		One Bertie S & T Corps evacuated sick	
VILLERS-FAUCON	30/11/17		One ASC ABC Von Driver HT evacuated sick MTC. Horse of 24 decks opened this morning & unit getting down into billets at 12:30 p.m. Received orders to saddle up & proceed forthwith to VILLERS FAUCON for active operations. Left FOURQUES at 2:30 p.m. arrived VILLERS FAUCON (about 15 miles) at 5 p.m. The ABC & Other horsemen and morales & animals about the same time. White horse bivouaced in a muddy field. (Off Coy)	

(Off Coy)

W.H. Coy
Murty Coy
E.C.t.O.E.H.

"Original"

(117)

CONFIDENTIAL

WAR DIARY
of
LUCKNOW CAVALRY FIELD AMBULANCE
for
MONTH of DECEMBER 1917.

VOLUME XXXV

COMMITTEE FOR THE
MEDICAL HISTORY OF THE WAR
Date 12 JUL 1918

WAR DIARY
or
INTELLIGENCE SUMMARY.

Army Form C. 2118.

Place	Date	Hour	Summary of Events and Information	Remarks and references to Appendices
VILLERS-FAUCON	1 Dec	4 a.m.	Orders received fr C.O. & Pack (mule) Ldr to report forthwith to K. Cav Div H.Q. as Brockm. Cav Bde had been temporarily attached to that Div.	
		6.30 am	'C.O.' & P.M.S (2 Offrs 6 O.R. + 10 animals (+ tack) started via ST EMILIE & EPEHY K Aus & B.W. H.Q. a brancart major info M ([F.S. SC.]) H.R.) Bn left early in front trailer. In the tank lad at dawn was with the whom Cav Bde fwd N of PEZIERES. Having shelled) C.O. (proceeded) on foot, from I Cav Div. 4.R about 8.30 a.m. & received news to forces with P.M.S. to report to Brockm. Cav Bde. H.Q. at VAVCELETTE FARM. C.O. returned to P.M.S. & PEZIERES – EPEHY and took them down to the FARM actors country. Found it impossible to get them mounts, so sent 1st Lieut Wyman back to VILLERS-FAUCON to bring up the "Beauvais" 9 on ambu. 3 horse ambulances and stretchers (now present) on foot to VAVCELETTE FARM, reported to G.O.C. v dis [known] starts fr Bde [kno] actly [drawn] Returned to P.M.S. & sent & truck to VILLERS & FAUCON again returned to kitchen Cav Bde H.Q. Stayed there till 2 p.m. under shell fire and [investigate] lieut Mother's party (wounded) Found 3 got over & women Least to HEUDICOURT. Then walked to HEUDICOURT and got the Division's horse ambulances to work. Evacuated wounded by wheeled stretchers & horse ambulance to HEUDICOURT, working in conjunction with other services [illeg] (Viz:- See C.F.A's Canadian C.F.A & Infantry &c.) At H.Q. HEUDICOURT the [wounded] were transferred to motor ambulances and sent to FINS.
			W.H. Cayley	

WAR DIARY or INTELLIGENCE SUMMARY

Army Form C. 2118.

Place	Date	Hour	Summary of Events and Information	Remarks and references to Appendices
	Dec 1 (cont)		At about 10 p.m. walked back to the (?) PPF at new VAUCELETTE FARM. Satisfied myself that all wounded from the front line had been brought to safety & evacuated up to Front Line. Made arrangements for evacuation of (?) wounded during the night & Returned to 9/20 Russian Gun Bde Workshops at HEUDICOURT arriving about midnight.	
VILLERS-FAUCON	Dec 2		Continued the evacuation of wounded still reported by scratch CFA bearers. Also the Russian Gun Bde. HQ & a few relieved during the night by Scottish Gun Bde. Rode to III Div HQ at EWA (624) & returned to VIIth Gun Bde had been relieved by IV Can Div Infy Bde and (?) P.m. left up returns from VILLERS-FAUCON (am) arrangement being been done while relieved by heavy fire of Sniper CFA. The weather, which was showering and turned colder. The districts west of reports & clear today. The activities in showing infantry opposite our wing at HEUDICOURT. The new numbered as in CFA columns at VILLERS-FAUCON.	
LE MESNIL	Dec 3		The whole 4 Can Div returned to Armies area. The Russ. CFA. (own batt'y + horses div march separately) were billeted in 2 horses. 2 III ARMY Hutts and 6 tents at Le Mesnil. Weather very wet. Shewing Gun Bde at LE MESNIL reminded at 1 hours notice to move. During these operations all routes of the Canes div including Asst. SANIYAL. I.M.S. & 1st Lieut WYMAN & RMC U.S.Army hospital very well acted. The Premier Gu of Russian RFA evacuated between 3/12 & 1/12 normally from wounded records.	

(H Clayngr?)

Army Form C. 2118

WAR DIARY
or
INTELLIGENCE SUMMARY.
(Erase heading not required.)

Place	Date	Hour	Summary of Events and Information	Remarks and references to Appendices
LE MESNIL	Dec 4th		Weather continues very cold with hard frost. Lucknow Cav Bde remains on 1 hours notice to move.	W.T.C.
"	Dec 5th		One Dvr r/m Beaver evacuated sick	W.T.C.
"			Still at one hours notice. Weather still very cold. Hosp. Stn Keeper Mohamed Sharif S/T Corp returned to base	W.T.C
"	Dec 6th		2 Beavers A.B.C. evacuated sick	W.T.C
"	"7"		1 Beaver A.B.C. no evacuated sick	W.T.C
"	"8"		A Pharos act in to-day after several days hard frost. One A.S.C. Driver rejoins from hospital. Unit on 1 hours notice to 48 hours from 6 p.m. to-day	W.T.C.
"	"9"		1 Beaver A.B.C. rejoins from hospital. One Driver A.S.C. M.T. joins as a reinforcement.	W.T.C
"	"10"		One Beaver A/B.C. evacuated sick. W.T.C. One R.A.M.C. man joins. Unit no check & on Reme man transferred to Adm.'s Office.	W.T.C.
"	"12"		One Beaver A/B.C. rejoins from hosp. 6 p.m. unit (less Beavers) on one hours notice to 72 hours	W.T.C.
"	13"		Lieut. Sanyal Inds T.C. & 3 O.Rs. detailed for temp.' duty with Lucknow Ca. B.	W.T. Crpy.g

WAR DIARY
or
INTELLIGENCE SUMMARY

Army Form C. 2118.

Place	Date	Hour	Summary of Events and Information	Remarks and references to Appendices
LE MESNIL	18/12/17		Had first frost last night. Heavy snow fall this night. Very cold. The accommodation in imperfect huts & tents is very trying to the Officers & men in this weather. One A.S.C. M.T. driver evacuated sick. W.M.C.	
"	19/12/17		One M.O. 1st Lieut. Wynne, with veterinary horse detached today for temporary duty with Can Corps H.Q. This leaves only myself & one Qual. with the Unit. W.M.C.	
ST CREN	20/12/17		The horses (F.A.) left. LE MESNIL today, and went into huts at ST CREN. Most of the huts had an occupancy by French troops but there is sufficient accommodation for all personnel and the housing is much better. The weather remains intensely cold.	
"	21/12/17		The Unit (less B. echelon) on 1 hour notice from 6 p.m. today, to 72 hours. W.M.C.	
"	23/12/17		One Sergt & two privates (men) as reinforcements as part of the 88th draft of Reinforcements. W.M.C.	

Army Form C. 2118.

WAR DIARY
or
INTELLIGENCE SUMMARY.
(Erase heading not required.)

Instructions regarding War Diaries and Intelligence Summaries are contained in F. S. Regs., Part II. and the Staff Manual respectively. Title pages will be prepared in manuscript.

Place	Date	Hour	Summary of Events and Information	Remarks and references to Appendices
ST OMER	24/12/17		Lieut. came off shown office hours at 9 from this evening	O.H.C
"	25/12/17		Two drivers A.S.C. M.T. arrived as reinforcements. Slight thaw today but weather still very wet	O.H.C
"	26/12/17		Frost again tonight.	O.H.C
"	27/12/17		On driver A.S.C. M.T. evacuated sick. A small party (1 Officer and 1 Radio Sect, 1 B. GR & 4 U.D.O.R) proceeded to the front line today to dig in a Bn working party. Seven drivers O.R.s (drivers) as reinforcements	O.H.C / O.H.C
"	30/12/17		A commencement made towards opening a Rest-Station for O.R.s & S[?]. Cas Evac. So far no money has been arranged owing to absence of stores in the bunks, so Butr today has hut placed with 30 bunks for orderlies.	O.H.C
"	31/12/17		The party returned from the front line. Weather still intensely cold & severe. Slight fall of snow last night & very hard frost.	

R.H. Boyd

Lucknow Gen. F. Ambce.

11. 3. 18

January 27th 1918.
February. 1918.

Original

(144)

"Miniature"

COMMITTEE FOR THE
MEDICAL HISTORY OF THE WAR
Date 12 JUL 1923

CONFIDENTIAL

War Diary of
Lucknow Cavalry Field Ambulance

for Month of January 1918.

Volume XXXVI.

Jan 1918.

Army Form C. 2118.

WAR DIARY
or
INTELLIGENCE SUMMARY.
(Erase heading not required.)

Instructions regarding War Diaries and Intelligence Summaries are contained in F.S. Regs., Part II. and the Staff Manual respectively. Title pages will be prepared in manuscript.

Place	Date	Hour	Summary of Events and Information	Remarks and references to Appendices
ST OMER	1/1/18		The Lucknow Q.F.A. is in quarters consisting of a farm house, an Armstrong Hut & 20 bivouac Huts. Two accommodation is also for 3 hospital. The horse lines are satisfactory & there are several improvised tents. The weather is very cold with short frosts & much snow. W.M.C.	
"	3/1/18		One British batman evacuated sick. W.M.C.	
"	4/1/18		A Rest Station for the H.T. & S. Coy Div who should happy are so far for 3rd Bn. Has 20 fr Br Batt. has entered so much that which all it 50. Horse kept up for a few batmen under S.V.C.	
"	5/1/18		One Officer & 6 O.R.s all from 2nd Canadian C.F.A. joined (temporary) 6 men to be R.v.S. Station. Also 2 Serbian labels junks W.M.C.	
"	6/1/18		Accommodation for British patients increases to 60 beds W.M.C.	
"	7/1/18		Lt George R.A.M.C. reported the Unit from temporary duty with M.17th Cas M.C. One case M.T. Driver (med) the Unit as a reinforcement W.M.C.	
"	8/1/18		Capt Cummy C.A.M.C. & his Batman left to rejoin their own Unit W.M.C.	
"	14/1/18		The weather is now warmer, thawing & raining	

W.M. Coy

Army Form C. 2118.

WAR DIARY
or
INTELLIGENCE SUMMARY.
(Erase heading not required.)

Place	Date	Hour	Summary of Events and Information	Remarks and references to Appendices
ST. CREN	18/1/16		Two British O.R.s evacuated sick. WTC	
"	20/1/16		Capt A.J. BENNEE R.A.M.C. joined the Unit from Amiens 36.A. With a view to replace Capt G. Jones about month as 2nd in Command. W.T.C. Sgt Major Robinson R.A.M.C. reported for duty with this Unit from No 11 C.C.S. & in relief of Sgt Major Moutgrien R.A.M.C. WTC Two A.B.C. men & one C.T.B. S/Sgt reported for duty W.T.C.	
"	22/1/16		The weather during the last week has been heavy & frosty. Fine throughout the day & keeps. W.T.C.	
"	24/1/16		One B.O.R. taken on to strength W.T.C.	
"	26/1/16		One Indian Hosp Storekeeper taken on to strength. W.T.C. Capt A.J. BENNEE R.A.M.C. Capt to unit having been transferred from 41 St'ty Hosp. He was not on the permanent strength. W.T.C.	
"	28/1/16		Capt H.J. KEANE R.A.M.C. (C.T.C.) reported for duty. W.T.C. One mule evacuated sick, keeps struck off the strength. W.T.C.	

W.H. Cr[...]

Army Form C. 2118.

WAR DIARY
or
INTELLIGENCE SUMMARY.
(Erase heading not required.)

Place	Date	Hour	Summary of Events and Information	Remarks and references to Appendices
ST CREN	29/1/18		Sgt Major M̶E̶ MUSGRAVE R.A.M.C. left the Unit for duty with No 11 C.C.S. and is struck off the strength. 10th C. Capt W. GRIFFITH JONES R.A.M.C. left to-day to report to War Office on the expiry of his contract and resignation of his commission W/O He is struck off the strength and Capt. H.J. KEANE R.A.M.C. is taken on the strength in his place.	
	31/1/18		Captain E.T. WYMAN V.S. M.R.C. was struck off the strength of the R.G.F.A. to-day having been posted to the 2nd Corps Div. The weather today during the last 5 or 6 days has been cold with frosts at night. It is now dull, rainy & thawing during the day time. W.H. Craig	

"Original" "Medical"

(194.)

War Diary of Lucknow
Cavalry Field Ambulance
for month of February 1918

Feb 1, 1918

VOLUME XXX

COMMITTEE FOR THE
MEDICAL HISTORY OF THE WAR
Date 12 JUL 1919

WAR DIARY
or
INTELLIGENCE SUMMARY.
(Erase heading not required.)

Army Form C. 2118.

Place	Date	Hour	Summary of Events and Information	Remarks and references to Appendices
ST CREN	1/2/18		One hand dav arrived in a reinforcement turns taken in to strength	WHC
"	3/2/18		One Transport Sergt Preveur F Bare (times in pris) & was struck off the strength	WHC
"	4/2/18		Lieut A R GEYER R.A.M.C. (T.C.) having been transferred to Luchnow C.C.S. was struck off the strength this day. Captain F. H. WOODS R.A.M.C. (T.C.) having joined this Unit for duty was taken on the strength this day.	WHC
MARCELCAVE	6/2/18		The Luchnow Cav. F.A. Amb. left St CREN this morning, marching at 9.30 A.M. arrived at MARCELCAVE at 4.15 P.M. The unit was billetted there for the night.	WHC
NAMPS-AU-MONT	7/2/18		The L. C.F.A. marched at 9.30 A.M. and arrived at NAMPS-AU-MONT at 5 P.M. The unit is billetted in the village. all horses were got under cover in French Stables, the wagons put into park at the side of the road. The mens' billets are not good to photograph & there is some misconception. There is a chateau in the village which is to be used as a hospital for Indians & the British Scabies cases.	WHC Caugh

Army Form C. 2118.

WAR DIARY
or
INTELLIGENCE SUMMARY.
(Erase heading not required.)

Instructions regarding War Diaries and Intelligence Summaries are contained in F. S. Regs., Part II. and the Staff Manual respectively. Title pages will be prepared in manuscript.

Place	Date	Hour	Summary of Events and Information	Remarks and references to Appendices
NAMPS-AU-MONT	8.2.18		One RAMC Private posted to this unit from the 5th inst, transferred from Div2 HQ	HJK
"	9.2.18		Lt Col Cagaly IMS proceeded on 14 days leave to England from 10th to 24th inst	HJK
"	11.2.18		One ASC MT proceeded on leave to England from 13th to 27th inst	HJK
"	12.2.18		One ASC MT struck off the strength of the unit, having been transferred to England with a view to gazetting for a commission	HJK
"	13.2.18		Capt S Thompson RAMC arrived for duty with this unit	HJK
"	16.2.18		HJK Arnat transferred to Australia CFA for duty	HJK
"			HSK Arnat from Australia CFA arrived for duty with this unit	HJK
"	21.2.18		Capt S Thompson RAMC transferred to Australia CFA for duty with Kathurst	HJK
"	"		Lt HABBECK USMRC arrived for duty with this unit	HJK
"	"		Two motor drivers proceeded on leave to UK from 21st Feb to 7th March	HJK
"	22.2.18		One motor driver proceeded on leave to UK from 22 Feb to 8th March	HJK
"	"		A Corpl Wheeler ASC HT rejoined this unit from the base	HJK
"	24.2.18		One B+S entrained on 24th inst and proceeded with a party going East	HJK
"	25.2.18		Lt Col Cagaly IMS rejoined from 14 days leave to UK	HJK

H.J. Keant
Captain

Army Form C. 2118.

WAR DIARY
INTELLIGENCE SUMMARY.
(Erase heading not required.)

Instructions regarding War Diaries and Intelligence Summaries are contained in F. S. Regs., Part II. and the Staff Manual respectively. Title pages will be prepared in manuscript.

Place	Date	Hour	Summary of Events and Information	Remarks and references to Appendices
NAMPS AU MONT	28/2/18		Lucknow Cav. Fd. Amb. begins its move to Egypt today. It is divided into three parties:— (a.) Main body — 1/Kro. (2nd i/c) 6 B.Os. 2 I.Os. 70 IORs. entrain today. (b.) The horse & motor transport under Capt Woogs to await orders & entrain about a week from now. (c.) A small advpt. party — Lt Sangul, 3 mtr ambulances with drivers & 5 IORs to remain till move of Troops is complete. In addition there are a few British details left who are now leave.	

W.H. Cray

1918
4TH CAVALRY DIVISION

104 MHOW ⎫ SIALKOT
COMBINED. CAVALRY FLD AMBS ⎬ MHOW
 ⎭ LUCKNOW

JAN - APL 1918

1917 FEB — 1918 MAR

to EGYPT 1 MOUNTED DIV
Trans

Sialkot
MHOW   } Cav. Fd. Ambs
Lucknow

Mhow Cav. Field Ambulance, 5th Cav. Division.

Feb 1917

COMMITTEE FOR THE
MEDICAL HISTORY OF THE WAR
Date 21 MAY 1917

Medical.   Serial No: **199**

Mhow Indian Cavalry Field Ambulance.

From 1st to 28th February 1917.

Army Form C. 2118.

WAR DIARY
or
INTELLIGENCE SUMMARY

(Erase heading not required.)

Officer Commanding
104th M.G. How. Indian Cavalry Field Ambulance

Army Form C. 2118.

Volume XXVIII

Instructions regarding War Diaries and Intelligence Summaries are contained in F.S. Regs., Part II. and the Staff Manual respectively. Title Pages will be prepared in manuscript.

Place	Date	Hour	Summary of Events and Information	Remarks and references to Appendices
BOUVAINCOURT	Feb 1st 1917		Horse Transport exercised - Took over duties of Divisional Hospital from Sect 3 M.G.F.A. Sgt CLEMENTS reported from for course at Divisional School.	
		9am	Fine cold day.	
do	Feb 2nd		Horse transport exercise. Physical training 2 am	
		9am	Fine cold day.	
do	Feb 3rd		Horse transport exercise - Physical training 2 am	
			Pay received revised	
		9am	Fine Cold day.	
do	Feb 4th		Horse parade 12.15 pm	
		9am	Fine cold day.	
do	Feb 5th		Horse transport exercised - Pack section entrenched 9 am - Physical training 2 pm	
			Capts E.A.C.MATTHEWS in board on S.S. OLIVIA HMS RAMC on wintly F.B board	
			Heavy snowstorm	
do	Feb 6th		Horse transport exercised - Physical training 2 pm	
			Sgt CARROLL on 10 days leave to U.K.	
		9am	Fine cold day.	
do	Feb 7th		Horse transport exercise Pack section entrenched 9am	
			Pte PRESSMAN returned from leave	
		9am	Fine cold day.	

Army Form C. 2118.

WAR DIARY
or
INTELLIGENCE SUMMARY

(Erase heading not required.)

Volume XXVIII

104 M.T. Coy. / C.T.R.

Place	Date	Hour	Summary of Events and Information	Remarks and references to Appendices
BOUVAINCOURT	Feb 8th		Horse transport section Reserved Personal fatigues. Harness inspection 11.30 am. One A.S.C. H.T. admitted sick. Fine frosty day.	
do	Feb 9th	Epleau	Horse transport received Pack section will attach 1 am Physical training & play. First aid demonstration to A.S.C. H.T. Commenced. Fine frosty day.	
do	Feb 10th	Dolen	Horse transport Reserved Personal fatigues - Physical training & games. One A.S.C. H.T. admitted sick. Pay returned received. Ration received for inspection of ambulance by M.A.C.A.D.S. Level. Fine cold day.	
do	Feb 11th	Epleau	Capt MATTHEWS R.A.M.C. rejoined from leave to U.K. One A.S.C. M.T. admitted sick. Fine frosty day.	
do	Feb 12th	Dolen	Horse transport received Personal fatigues. Lieut G.A. MENON I.M.S. to left for England on termination of service. Lieut CROIK R.A.M.C. rejoined from temporary duty with 8th Howitzer Bde. A.S.C.H.T. admitted sick. Harness & van cleaned. Fine cold day.	

Army Form C. 2118.

WAR DIARY
or
INTELLIGENCE SUMMARY

(Erase heading not required.)

Vol XXVIII p.3

Instructions regarding War Diaries and Intelligence Summaries are contained in F.S. Regs., Part II. and the Staff Manual respectively. Title Pages will be prepared in manuscript.

Place	Date	Hour	Summary of Events and Information	Remarks and references to Appendices
BOUVINCOURT	Feb 13th		Horse transport exercised. Personnel fatigues. Lt. M.L. BHAGAT I.M.S. T.C. Transferred to 8 G. Hospital ROUEN	
do	Calm		Fair cold day	
do	Feb 14th		Horse transport exercised. Personnel fatigues. Lt. ADC H.T. now APO M.T. returned from hospital. One horse also returned from WERNON C.C.S.	
do	Calm		Fair cold day	
do	Feb 15th		Horse transport exercised. Personnel fatigues. One horse APO admitted sick.	
do	Calm		Dull cold day. Thaw'd	
do	Feb 16th		Horse transport exercised. Personnel fatigues. One APO H.T. admitted sick.	
do	Calm		Dull cold day	
do	Feb 17th		Inspection of ambulance by M.A.C. 5th Cas Divn 10.15 am. Pay received — received. One horse APO transferred to No C.C.S.	
do	Calm		Dull cold day	

Army Form C. 2118.

WAR DIARY
or
INTELLIGENCE SUMMARY

Volume XX VIII   p 4.
(Erase heading not required.)   OC 104 MT Coy (CT)

Instructions regarding War Diaries and Intelligence Summaries are contained in F. S. Regs., Part II. and the Staff Manual respectively. Title Pages will be prepared in manuscript.

Place	Date	Hour	Summary of Events and Information	Remarks and references to Appendices
BEAUMESNIL	Feb. 18th	Before Dawn	Church parade 6 a.m. Fine day.	
do	Feb. 19th	—	Horse Transport received personal fatigues — Park section paraded 9.30am. Inspection of Park section by DDMS 3 Cav. Bgde 3.15 p.m. Thaw setting started.	
	Dawn		Dull misty day.	
do	Feb. 20th		Horse Transport received — personal fatigues. FrieT and administration for holiday accounted. One bomb A.S.C. reported from 2 C.C.S. One A.S.C. H.T. reported from [illegible] division. One Capt H.T. admitted sick.	
	DayOn		Dull day.	
do	Feb. 21st		Horse Transport received — personal fatigues — Park section paraded 9.30 am. One ASC H.T. returned from hospital. Two ASC H.T. transferred to auxiliary Horse Transport Co. Major MATHEWSON temporarily duty as DAQMG 3rd Cav. Div.	
	After		Dull day.	
do	Feb. 22nd		Horse transport received personal fatigues. Park section paraded. Lt. C. RUDSHANK on temporary duty with 71st Division Train. One ASC H.T. evacuated sick.	
	Later		Dull day.	

Army Form C. 2118.

WAR DIARY
or
INTELLIGENCE SUMMARY

Volume XXVIII   195.   O.C. 104 M70w/102_

(Erase heading not required.)

Place	Date	Hour	Summary of Events and Information	Remarks and references to Appendices
BOSINGHOURT	Feb 23rd	Dawn	Horse transport exercised - personnel fatigues - Pack section parade 11.30am for S.A. Drill Gas Goggles	
do	Feb 24th	Dawn	Dull day	
			Horse transport exercised - personnel fatigues - Physical training 2 pms	
do	Feb 25th	Dawn	Pay received - issued	
		Dusk	Fine day	
do	Feb 26th	Dawn	Horse transport exercised - personnel fatigues - pack section shield 9.30am	
			Physical training 2 pm	
			Pte LETHBY returned from leave	
do	Feb 27th	Dawn	Horse transport exercised - personnel fatigues - pack section shield 9.30am	
			Physical training 2 pm	
			Capt J.G. FIRTH RAMC (SR) posted for duty	
			Sgt CARROLL returned from leave	
			Dull day	
do	Feb 28th	Dawn	Horse transport exercised - personnel fatigues - pack section shield 9.30am	
			Dull cold day	

W. Cruickshank Major
Comdg 104 M70w/1 Gt

Mhow box 1. a.

COMMITTEE FOR THE
MEDICAL HISTORY OF THE WAR
Date -6 JUL. 1917

Army Form C. 2118.

WAR DIARY
or
INTELLIGENCE SUMMARY

VOLUME XXIX

(Erase heading not required.) 1/4 M+qvr Indian Cavalry Field Ambulance

O-C

Instructions regarding War Diaries and Intelligence Summaries are contained in F.S. Regs., Part II and the Staff Manual respectively. Title Pages will be prepared in manuscript.

Place	Date	Hour	Summary of Events and Information	Remarks and references to Appendices
BOUVAINCOURT	March 1/19		Horse transport exercised — Duties of divisional Hospital handed over	(SEE 1347)
			I.C.7.A. On ADO H.T. admitted sick. Physical Training 2.30pm	
	Solvy		Fine day.	
do	March 2nd		Horse transport exercised. Personnel fatigues. Physical Training 2.30pm	
	Solvy		Fine day.	
do	March 3rd		Horse transport exercised. Personnel fatigues. Physical Training 2.30pm	
			Pay received	
	Solvy		Fine day.	
do	March 4th		Church parade 6 p.m.	
	Solvy		Fine day.	
do	March 5th		Horse transport exercised. 6 stretcher bearers from 9th H.H. & 6 from 1st Lancers joined for instruction in Field section work. Field Section parade 9.30 am	
			Capt MATTHEW S on medical board for P.B. men.	
			Physical training 2 p.m. Lecture on work. Company drill 9.30 am Stretcher drill 2.30 pm On ADO H.T. rejoined from hospital.	
	Solvy		Dull day	
do	March 6th		Horse transport exercised. Field section parade 9.30 am Physical training 2.30 pm	
			Indian bank stretcher drill 9.30 am Company drill 2.30 pm	
	Solvy		Cold day	

WAR DIARY
or
INTELLIGENCE SUMMARY

Army Form C. 2118.

Vol XXIX

(Erase heading not required.)

O.C. for
104 MHOW I.C.I.G.

Place	Date	Hour	Summary of Events and Information	Remarks and references to Appendices
BOUVANCOURT	March 7th		Horse transport received Pack saddles, parade 9.30 am. Physical Training & firing interior knock, company drill 9.30 am. Stretcher drill & inspection. Cold day.	
do	March 8th		Horse transport received. Personal fatigues. Major MATTHEWS returned from offg D.A.Q.M.S. Heavy snow shower.	
do	March 9th		Horse transport received. Personal fatigues. Dull day.	
do	March 10th		Pack section parade 9.30 am. Preliminary inspection, company drill 9.30 am. stretcher drill 2.30 pm. Physical training. M.T. return as before. Pay received material from dump.	
do	March 11th		Horse parade 12.45 pm. Dull day.	
do	March 12th		Horse Transport received. Stretcher work, company drill 9.30 am. Stretcher drill 2.30 pm. Fine day.	

Army Form C. 2118.

WAR DIARY or INTELLIGENCE SUMMARY

(Erase heading not required.)

Army Form C. 2118.

Place	Date	Hour	Summary of Events and Information	Remarks and references to Appendices
BOURDON	March 13th		Horse transport exercised. Orders received for the Brigade to move at 4.8 hours notice. Showery day.	
do	March 14th		Horse transport exercised. Medical inspection all ranks. 23 O.R. Capt MATTHEWS to Base & Paris. Inspection of equipment, gas hood inspection N.T. to form. Dental detail, physical training, games.	
do	March 15th		Horse transport exercised. Route march, dismounted ranks 9 a.m. Dull day.	
do	March 16th		Field day advanced rear guard action. Dull day.	
do	March 17th		Horse transport exercised. Indian tank, physical drill 9.30 a.m. Brunier inspection during Stables. Party under 2nd Lt. ARMA from AMARA proceeded Latrines approved. 3 men ambulance conveying sick to ROUEN from LUCKNOW C.C.S. Pay received.	
			Fine day.	
do	March 18th		Church Parade 6 a.m. Capt MATTHEWS returned from leave to PARIS. Showery day.	

WAR DIARY or INTELLIGENCE SUMMARY

Army Form C. 2118.

Vol XXIV p. 4 Aug.
10.4.1.0.3.A

Place	Date	Hour	Summary of Events and Information	Remarks and references to Appendices
BOUVINCOURT	March 19th	10am	Orders received to move East on 20th to be at rendezvous at 10.30 am. Showery day.	
SIGNARPONT	March 20th	10am	Ambulance marched from BOUVINCOURT at 9.30am, arrived in SIGNARPONT at 4pm. Cold windy day.	
REVELLES	March 21st	10am	Ambulance marched from SIGNARPONT at 9.45 am, arrived at REVELLES at 3.15pm. Snow showers, very cold.	
CAGNY	March 22nd	10am	Ambulance marched from REVELLES at 10am, arrived at CAGNY at 5.30pm. Orders received that the ambulance is placed under orders of G.O.C. AMBALA Cav Bde. Cold day, snow showers.	
BOIS de MERSAUCOURT	March 23rd		Ambulance marched from CAGNY at 2pm, & joined AMBALA Cav Bde at BOIS de MERSAUCOURT 7.30pm. Orders received to march with A Lahore Division on MERSAUCOURT. Advanced Dressing Station at PROUILLES & Tent Section at FALVY. Fine cold day.	
PRUSLES	March 24th		Advanced Dressing Station marched at 8.15am, arrived & opened at PRUSLES at 12 noon. Tent Section marched at 8.15am arrived at FALVY at 10.30 pm. On way in roads indented were found blocked & bridges destroyed, a very bad situation could not be taken. Fine frosty day.	

Army Form C. 2118.

WAR DIARY
or
INTELLIGENCE SUMMARY
(Erase heading not required.)

Instructions regarding War Diaries and Intelligence Summaries are contained in F. S. Regs., Part II. and the Staff Manual respectively. Title Pages will be prepared in manuscript.

Place	Date	Hour	Summary of Events and Information	Remarks and references to Appendices
PROSLES	March 25th		Tent Section rejoined advanced dressing section at PROSLES. Wire reception of casualty 4 p.m. Admitted total 1 B.O. 600 rounded 2 I.O.R. all dressed & 4/1/4.S. MIDLAND R.A. & PERSONNG orders received for future evacuation to be	
do	March 26th		Shelter trench half lightening section cleared ready to move forward. Advanced. Admitted wounded 4 I.O. wounded 4 I.O.R. 3 evacuated.	
do	March 27th		Snowy wet day. Advanced dressing section moved to TINCOURT. Admitted wounded B.O. 2 B.O.R. 17 evacuated	
do	March 28th		Advanced dressing station rejoined at PROSLES. Admitted wounded B.O.R. 1 evacuated. When received a probable minor concussion. Quiet snowy day.	
Bois de MENOUCOURT	March 29th		Handed over PROSLES at 12.30 p.m. marched to BOIS de MENOUCOURT 6 p.m. Orders received for an Rav & Officer to exchange duties with Of WORLEY Ranks of the Supply Column 5t Car Div. Open to Rayelem of sect. Very wet day.	

Army Form C. 2118.

Vol XXIX p. 6.

WAR DIARY
or
INTELLIGENCE SUMMARY
(Erase heading not required.)

WW MTW 1072.

Place	Date	Hour	Summary of Events and Information	Remarks and references to Appendices
WARFUSÉE-ABANCOURT	March 31		Marched from BOIS du MEREAUCOURT at 11.15 am, arrived at WARFUSÉE-ABANCOURT at 3 pm. Capt. J.M. FIRTH R.A.M.C. reported his departure to Supply Column 6th and 8rd div. Capt. W.E.A. WORLEY R.A.M.C joined from there for duty. Open for reception of sick.	
	April 1st		Wet day	
do	April 2		Rest	
			Showery day	

L Quibet Laurt
Lieut Col
a.d. 199 M.T.W. 1.O.T.W.

2449 Wt. W14957/M90 750,000 1/16 J.B.C. & A. Forms/C.2118/12.

COMMITTEE FOR THE MEDICAL HISTORY OF THE WAR
Date −6 JUL. 1917

Mhow cav. F.A.

April 1917
5

WAR DIARY
or
INTELLIGENCE SUMMARY

Army Form C. 2118.

Vol 28

Volume XXX

(Erase heading not required.) 104 M How British Cavalry Field Ambulance

Instructions regarding War Diaries and Intelligence Summaries are contained in F. S. Regs., Part II. and the Staff Manual respectively. Title Pages will be prepared in manuscript.

Place	Date	Hour	Summary of Events and Information	Remarks and references to Appendices
WARFUSEE ABAINCOURT	April 1st 1917 Dawn		Rest. Showery day.	
do	April 2nd		Horse transport received. Personnel fatigues. Inspection of troops & equipment. Fine day.	
do	April 3rd Dawn		Horse transport received. Personnel fatigues. Working party. Heavy snow storm.	
do	April 4th		Personnel fatigues. Snow storm.	
do	April 5th Dawn		Horse transport received. Personnel fatigues. Fine day.	
do	April 6th Dawn		Horse transport received. Personnel fatigues. Two Ford ambulances received from No. 2 Sunbeam sent to S.E."B"A.D.I.C.T.a. Cold windy day.	
do	April 7th		Horse transport received. Personnel fatigues. Orders received to be at 5 hours notice to move from midnight 7th-8th & will probably be evacuated. Pay received.	

Army Form C. 2118.

WAR DIARY
or
INTELLIGENCE SUMMARY

Vol XXX

(Erase heading not required.)

Place	Date	Hour	Summary of Events and Information	Remarks and references to Appendices
WARFUSEE ABAINCOURT	April 8th		Church Parade 6.30 pm. Very fine day.	
do	April 9th		Horse transport arrived - killing received road march 9 am. Stables, kit inspection. Heavy snow shower.	
do	April 10th		Horse transport arrived A.B.C. Stretcher drill 9 am. Cold showery day.	
do	April 11th		Horse transport arrived. Indian ranks physical drill 9.30 am. Cold snowy day.	
do	April 12th		Horse transport arrived - Indian ranks route march 9 am. Cold day.	
do	April 13th		Horse transport arrived - Indian personnel fatigues. Orders received to march eastward on 14th. Pay received manual. Cold showery day.	
COULAINCOURT	April 14th		Ambulance marched from WARFUSEE-ABAINCOURT in rear of No.5 C.O. Edd at 7 am to COULAINCOURT arriving at 6.30 pm. Very fine day.	

Army Form C. 2118.

WAR DIARY
INTELLIGENCE SUMMARY

(Erase heading not required.)

Instructions regarding War Diaries and Intelligence Summaries are contained in F.S. Regs., Part II. and the Staff Manual respectively. Title Pages will be prepared in manuscript.

Vol XX No. 3   O/C   C.O. M/4 W I C Fa.

Place	Date	Hour	Summary of Events and Information	Remarks and references to Appendices
COULAINCOURT	April 15th		Reinforcement horses received — three light draught horses transferred to A.M.B.369	
		Day	Mobile Veterinary Section.	
			Very wet day.	
do	April 16th		Horse transport returned. Personnel fatigues.	
		Day	Paid S/Sgt CLEMENTS posted to H.Q. III Corps	
			Showery day.	
do	April 17th		Horse transport returned. Personnel fatigues.	
		Day	A/Sgt CARROLL A.P.C. M.T. posted to H.Q. IV Corps.	
			Showery day.	
do	April 18th		Horse transport returned. Personnel fatigues.	
		Day	Pte COTTON C4 W.S. posted from H.Q. 5th Cav Bgde	
			Wet day.	
do	April 19th		Horse transport received. Personnel fatigues.	
		Day	Dull mild day.	
do	April 20th		Bugle unmusick knit transport received. Personnel fatigues	
		Day	Dull cold day.	

Army Form C. 2118.

WAR DIARY
or
INTELLIGENCE SUMMARY
(Erase heading not required.)

Vol XXX

Place	Date	Hour	Summary of Events and Information	Remarks and references to Appendices
Oourthecourt	April 21st		Horse transport exercise. Personnel fatigues. Fire brazier against the hut.	
	April 22nd		Part received material. Church Parade 6 pm.	
			Rest.	
	April 23rd		Horse transport exercise. Personnel fatigues.	
			Rest day.	
	April 24		Brigade field day (Cancelled) drawing section out.	
	April 25		Rest day.	
			Horse transport exercise. Personnel fatigues.	
			No brass bounded pick.	
			Rest day.	
	April 26		Horse transport exercise. Personnel fatigues.	
			Rest day.	
Valen	April 27		Horse transport exercise. Personnel fatigues.	
			Two vehicles etc evacuated pick.	
			One third cook moved from base.	
			Rest day.	

Army Form C. 2118.

WAR DIARY
INTELLIGENCE SUMMARY

(Erase heading not required.)

Vol XXX

of 184 M[?]

Place	Date	Hour	Summary of Events and Information	Remarks and references to Appendices
COULAINCOURT	April 28th		Route march and personal fatigues. Pay received received during the day.	
do	April 29th		Each Church parade held 6 am. Remainder of day.	
do	April 30th		Horse transport reviewed. Personal fatigues during the day.	

W. Winterfield
Major (?)
O.C 184 M[?] C/33

Mhow Ind. Cav. Field Ambulance.

COMMITTEE FOR THE
MEDICAL HISTORY OF THE WAR
Date 27.IIII.1917

Army Form C. 2118.

WAR DIARY

Volume XXIX

INTELLIGENCE SUMMARY.

(Erase heading not required.)

104 M How Indian Cavalry Field Ambulance

Instructions regarding War Diaries and Intelligence Summaries are contained in F. S. Regs., Part II. and the Staff Manual respectively. Title pages will be prepared in manuscript.

Place	Date	Hour	Summary of Events and Information	Remarks and references to Appendices
COULAINCOURT	1917 May 1st		Horse transport exercise — Personnel fatigues. LtSNODGRASS one man of 14th M.G.S. evacuated to Pasteur Institute PARIS for anti-rabic treatment. Both were bitten by a mad dog belonging to an officer of the 14th. The dog which was destroyed by the Veterinary department was pronounced by a Veterinary Officer as suffering from what one also N.T. admitted rabies.	
do	May 2nd		Very hot day. Personnel fatigues, Inspection of horse transport together with Vet. of AM 34th Cav. Bde at 3pm by M.F.C. 5th Cav Divn who remarked that the horses were the best turned out unit in the Brigade.	
do	May 3rd		Very hot day. Horse transport exercise. Personnel fatigues. One man in one of 14.45.14 G.S. sent to PARIS for anti-rabic treatment under the same circumstances as those on May 1st. Extremely hot day.	
do	May 4th		Horse transport exercise. Personnel fatigues. P5 KIRWIN RAMC transferred to No 13 M.G.S. One ADC NOT returned from hospital. Excessive hot day.	

2353 Wt. W2544/1454 700,000 5/15 L.D.D.&L. A.D.S.S./Forms/C. 2118.

Army Form C. 2118.

Instructions regarding War Diaries and Intelligence Summaries are contained in F. S. Regs., Part II. and the Staff Manual respectively. Title pages will be prepared in manuscript.

WAR DIARY
INTELLIGENCE SUMMARY.
(Erase heading not required.)

Vol. XX. P.2
104 M How'l l. C. 2 a

Place	Date	Hour	Summary of Events and Information	Remarks and references to Appendices
COULLAINCOURT	May 5th		Horse transport received. Personnel fatigues.	
			3 between A.B.O. left for base as unfit for further service at the front.	
			Pay received.	
	Do		Fine hot day. Rain at night.	
do	May 6th		Recd. Rev Father McCann (F.C.R.C.) joined.	
			One N.C.O. + 10 men of 5th Cav Sanitary Section arrived for duty for cleaning up	
			the brigade area.	
	Do		Fine cool day.	
do	May 7th		Horse transport received. Personnel fatigues. Revd Father John Leary will be attending joined	
	Do		Fine day.	
do	May 8th		Horse transport received. Personnel fatigues.	
			Revd Father McCann reported him departure for 4th Can where Pte REID a/Sgt admitted hosp	
	Do		Hot day.	
do	May 9th		Horse transport received. Personnel fatigues.	
			Medical inspection all ranks.	
	Do		Hot day	

Army Form C. 2118.

WAR DIARY
or
INTELLIGENCE SUMMARY.
(Erase heading not required.)

Vol XXXI A.3. O.C.
1/74 MITFW / C.F.A.

Place	Date	Hour	Summary of Events and Information	Remarks and references to Appendices
CAUDRECOURT	May 10th		Horse transport service. Personal fatigues. Thursday day.	
do	May 11th		Horse transport service. Personal fatigues. S.S. SHEPHERD intelligence. Information received. Yummy day.	
do	May 12th		Horse transport service. Personal fatigues. Pay received received. After Hot Thursday day.	
do	May 13th		Rest. One L.D. while received from 9th Bde. Hot thursday day.	
do	May 14th		Horse transport service. Personal fatigues. Orders received to act as a tent section to the Canadian Divisional Brigade whose advanced dressing section is provided by its Canadian C.F.A. and situated at VADENCOURT (R16 a 9.4. Map 1. 40,000 62 £ S.E.) Transport in provided by them. Qtr BENTLEY A.P.C.M.T admitted sick.	In march in unopened 220 4pt-E r 11
			Dallen Friday day.	

Army Form C. 2118.

WAR DIARY
or
INTELLIGENCE SUMMARY.

(Erase heading not required.)

Vol XXXI p 4

1076 M/HW 10 Fu

Instructions regarding War Diaries and Intelligence Summaries are contained in F. S. Regs., Part II. and the Staff Manual respectively. Title pages will be prepared in manuscript.

Place	Date	Hour	Summary of Events and Information	Remarks and references to Appendices
RAVENSCOURT	May 15th		Three transport recruits Received fatigue	
			Duties	
do	May 16th		Three transport recruits. Personnel fatigue. Capt J. A. MACLEAN & one Private Ravine left for temporary duty with SECBAOLC 7.A.	
do	Sunday		Free day.	
do	May 17th		Three transport recruits. Received fatigue one BOR admitted wounded reverted.	
	Enemy		Shewing day	
do	May 18th		Three transport recruits. Received fatigue. 6 between ABC left for temporary duty with advanced Dressing Station. SEC BAO L Cpl L Cpl Russeyn reported from leave & England. 3 BOR admitted wounded reverted.	
	Enemy		Free day	
do	May 19th		Three transport recruits. Personnel fatigue. Cpl BENNET reported from hospital.	

2353 Wt. W2544/1454 700,000 5/15 D. D. & L. A.D.S.S./Forms/C. 2118.

Army Form C. 2118.

WAR DIARY
or
INTELLIGENCE SUMMARY.
(Erase heading not required.)

VOL XXXI p 5
10th Mtd Fd Amb

Instructions regarding War Diaries and Intelligence Summaries are contained in F.S. Regs., Part II and the Staff Manual respectively. Title pages will be prepared in manuscript.

Place	Date	Hour	Summary of Events and Information	Remarks and references to Appendices
ONVILLERS MENIL			Pay received — 2 B.O.R. admitted wounded remained	
			Clean Showery day	
do	May 20th		Church parade 6.30 pm	
			Col Bent & A.D.M.S left for Inspection & looking up a temporary entrainment R.H.	
			Clear Showery day —	
do	May 21st		Horse transport received personal fatigues	
			Tent section with A.D. took stock, but actual inspection before an enemy first Reconnaissance	
			to horse decoy station for Canadian wounded Brigade and local details.	
			One personnel Record received from SCC BAD 10 am	
			1 B.O. & 3 B.O.R. admitted wounded remained	
			Clear wet day —	
do	May 22nd		Horse transport received personal fatigues —	
			1 B.O.R. received wounded passed to horse decoy station	
			Clear wet day —	

Army Form C. 2118.

WAR DIARY
or
INTELLIGENCE SUMMARY.

(Erase heading not required.)

Vol XXII

No 6
65th Mtd / C. F.D.

Instructions regarding War Diaries and Intelligence
Summaries are contained in F. S. Regs., Part II.
and the Staff Manual respectively. Title pages
will be prepared in manuscript.

Place	Date	Hour	Summary of Events and Information	Remarks and references to Appendices
Cavanagh	May 23rd		Three transport received. Personnel fatigues one O.D. made evacuated - wounded admitted evacuated 1 B.O.R. D.D.M.S. Cavalry Corps inspected the hospital arrangements	to change in hospital arrangements See App IV.
do	May 24		Fine day. Three transport received - Personnel fatigues wounded admitted evacuated 3 B.O.R	
do	May 25th		Fine day. Huge transport received - Personnel fatigues wounded admitted evacuated 1 B.O.R	
Cavan			Shower day.	
do	May 26th		Three transport received. Personnel fatigues wounded admitted evacuated 3 B.O.R. One been appointed sick. Pay received received. Capt J.A.M.McEan rejoined from J.C.O.'BAD / C.F.O	For conveyance of sick See App V
Cavan			Shower day	

WAR DIARY or INTELLIGENCE SUMMARY.

Army Form C. 2118.

by XXX) O.C
14 N/oW/C.7.a

Place	Date	Hour	Summary of Events and Information	Remarks and references to Appendices
COURCELLES	May 27th	Noon	Arrived Reed	
			Unloaded & shuttled forwarded 2 B.O.R. & Reinforced 2 mules received	
do	May 28th		Easier than day.	
			Two lorry parties/Reinforced fatigues	
	Relief		Easier than day.	
do	May 29th		This being quiet Reported for duty	
			Capt MATTHEWS proceeded to S.E.P. B.A.D. (?) Reserved tracks in advance of JEANCOURT in persuant of rearward road	
			Three 12" shell fell in village about 7:15 pm men in W.G.S. shelter	
do	May 30th		Quite the day.	
			Hers important news — Personnel fatigues	
			Sgt End SHEPHERD upwards from 14th Reserve Park	
do	May 31st		First day's work / Shuttle reworked B.O.1. B.O.R.G.	
			Then transport service Personnel fatigues	
			The mules evacuated L.M.V.S.	

Army Form C. 2118.

WAR DIARY
or
INTELLIGENCE SUMMARY.
(Erase heading not required.)

Vol XXXI

WE
(6 U M H W / O Ld

Instructions regarding War Diaries and Intelligence Summaries are contained in F. S. Regs., Part II. and the Staff Manual respectively. Title pages will be prepared in manuscript.

Place	Date	Hour	Summary of Events and Information	Remarks and references to Appendices
CAULINCOURT	Sept 3rd		Major A YOUNG returned from leave to U.K. Major MATTHEWS proceeded on 28 day Canadian Leave to U.K. to see his General Dressing Station replenished and put into use to take up over next weeks. Inoculation for the unit for the month T.A.B. 100 70 --	

D. Winterton
Major RCA.
Cmdg No 10 W L 8 Div

Appendix I

CANADIAN C.F.A.

1. The Advanced Dressing Station of this unit will take over the Advanced Dressing Station at VADENCOURT (R.16.a.9.4) on the 14th inst. Advanced party to arrive at noon that day, remainder moving in the same evening at dusk. All wheeled transport less 1 Motor Ambulance to return to VERMOND. Officer Commanding MHOW I CFA will place 4 wheeled Stretcher Carriers at disposal of O.C. CANADIAN C.F.A. for use with the Advanced Dressing Station. Regimental Aid Posts at R.11.a.8.4. Hand Carriage of Casualties by wheeled Stretcher Carriers to Advanced Dressing Station. Thence by Motor Ambulance to MHOW I CFA at CAULAIN COURT. O.C. A.D. Station of CANADIAN C.F.A. will evacuate any casualties of 35th Division occurring before the reliefs are completed to the Fd: Ambulance of that Division at VERMAND. Tent Section, CANADIAN CFA will open at MONCHY-LAGACHE for treatment of sick of remainder of CANADIAN CAV: Bde: and will also collect sick from Divl: Amm: Col:, Aux H.T. Company, Fd: Squad R.E, at TERTRY, and from Divl: Supply Column.

2. MHOW I CFA
   will stand fast and will collect and treat sick from remainder of SEC'BAD and AMBALA Brigades, Divl: Reserve Park and Lumbered Train, and will also be prepared to admit casualties from Ad: Dressing Station, CANADIAN C.F.A, and slight cases of Indian wounded from St: CREN.

3. Route of evacuation of sick and wounded

Appendix II

Situation of other Medical Units.

No: 21 Motor Ambulance Convoy, PERONNE (Q.1.27.6.8.7.)

III rd Corps Rest Station, CERISY, (Q.2.d.2.0., Sheet 62.d)

Fourth Army Medical Units to be utilised by Cav: Corps.

Cas: Clg: Stations No: 5. BRAY, for sick.
No: 34, PERONNE-LA-CHAPELLETTE, for wounded.
No: 55. ————— do —————
No: 13. GAILLY, for cases of shell concussion, nervous shock, and doubtful gassed cases.
No: 13, GAILLY, for self-inflicted wound cases
No: 38 HEILLY, for infectious cases.

LUCKNOW Cas: Clg: Station. BRAY (shortly to move to PERONNE-LA-CHAPELLETTE).

Stationary Hospital No: 1. NEW ZEALAND Stationary Hospital AMIENS (officers Hospital and for Eye cases)

Advanced Depots of Medical Stores No: 32. Advanced Depot of Medical Stores GAILLY.

No: 3. Mobile X-Ray unit attached No: 34 Cas: Clg: Station, PERONNE-LA-CHAPELLETTE.

Mobile Laboratories:—

No: 10. Mobile Laboratory (Bac:) BRAY.
No: 11   "   "   (Bac:) HEILLY.
No: 12   "   "   (Hyg) PERONNE

Appendix III

Under instructions received from the D.D.M.S., Cavalry Corps returns from the Main Dressing Station of the Division only are required. You will therefore close your "A" and "D" book from noon to-day keeping a record for your own information only, but not in the "A" and "D" Book.

All cases now in your C.F.A. will be shewn as transferred, on paper, as from noon to-day to the Main Dressing Station, for inclusion in the "A" and "D" Book of that Unit.:—

By 8. a.m. daily the number of cases "remained" "discharged" &c. will also be furnished to O.C. Main Dressing Station for inclusion in his daily State.

By 8. a.m. also, intimation to O.C. Main Dressing Station will be given of the number of cases, British and Indian separately, requiring evacuation, and their categories; e.g.:—

5 Sick, 2 wounded, 5 Scabies, 20 Rose Measles &c.

All cases for evacuation should reach the M.D.S. by 10-30. a.m. daily for conveyance to Cas: Cleargᵍ Station &c. by Ambulance Convoy.

Numbers of wounded as per pro-forma attached will be furnished to O.C., M.D.S. by 5-30. A.M. and 8-30. P.M. daily for incorporation in the wire to D.D.M.S, Cav'y Corps.

Appendix IV
Medical Arrangements CAV: CORPS

1. Medical Organisation

(a) With the view to centralisation of medical arrangements and to facilitate evacuations by Motor Ambulance Convoy, the corps area will be divided into two sectors, the left sector that to be held by the 2nd and 3rd Cavalry Divisions, and the right sector that to be held by the 4th and 5th Cavalry Divisions.

In each sector one main Dressing Station only will be organised for the reception of sick and wounded: for the left sector at VILLERS FAUCON, and for the right sector in the neighbourhood of BERNES. The latter will be organised for the reception of British and Indian Troops.

(b) Advanced Dressing Stations will be organised as required in Divisional areas by ADsMS concerned.

(c) A Corps Rest Station for British Troops will be established at DOINGT, and a Corps Rest Station for Indian troops at St: CREN.

ADsMS in the sectors referred to will make mutual arrangements as to the units and personnel required for the M.D. Stations and Corps Rest Stations above detailed.

(d) Subsidiary Ambulance Stations for the treatment of slight cases for a few days will be opened as sparingly as possible.

Divisional Rest Stations will be discontinued as soon as the Corps Rest Station at DOINGT and the Indian Rest Station at St. CREN are organised.

No further cases will be sent to the Divl. R. Station at VILLERS CARBONNEL or to the III Corps Convalescent Depot at CERISY.

(e) British sick and wounded of the Cav: Corps will be evacuated to Nos: 36 and 39 C.C.Ss. at TINCOURT from the 23rd instant, with certain exceptions as detailed in 2.

Indian sick and wounded will be evacuated to the LUCKNOW C.C.S. at PERONNE LA CHAPELLETTE from the 23rd instant.

(1)

(f) Evacuations from M.D.Ss and Corps Rest Stations to C.C.Ss will be carried out by No: 36 Motor Amb: Convoy which is to be located within the chateau grounds at TINCOURT. In the meantime evacuations will continue by No: 21 Motor Amb: Convoy.

2. **Arrangements for Special Cases**

Officers
Dental cases (details of attendance will be resumed later)
Cases for X-Ray examination
Venereal cases
} British Troops to Nos 36 and 39 Casualty Cl: Stations at TINCOURT.

Infectious cases other than Rose Measles — No: 38 C.C.S HEILLY

Rose Measles — Corps Rest Station, DOINGT.

Self-inflicted wounds
Shell shock and allied conditions
"Gassed" cases
} No: 41 Stationary Hospl, GAILLY in relief of No: 13 C.C.S from 23" instant.

Eye cases of special nature and cases requiring to be seen by the ophthalmic Specialist } No: 59 General Hospital, AMIENS

3. **Indian Troops. Officers and Other Ranks**

All ordinary cases sick and wounded and all special cases as above mentioned, will be evacuated to the LUCKNOW C.C.S. at PERONNE LA CHAPELLETTE, from the 23rd instant.

4. **Advanced Depot of Medical Stores**

No: 14 Advanced Depot of Medical Stores is open at TINCOURT and will supply units and formations of the Cavalry Corps.

Appendix V

Copy of D.D.M.S. Cav. Corps No. M/10/8 d/25/5/17.

The Fourth Army Ophthalmic Centre at AMIENS is closing on 25th instant, and moving to PERONNE.

The Ophthalmic Centre will reopen on Wednesday 30th instant at the Civil Hospital, PERONNE.

This cancels the reference to Eye cases being sent to AMIENS in my orders operations No: 3 dated 23/5/17.

The following will be the arrangements for special eye cases.

Eye-cases (British troops) of special nature and cases requiring to be seen by the Ophthalmic Specialist will be assembled once a week on Wednesdays at 9 a.m. at the Corps Rest Stations at DOINGT and at St CREN. Nominal rolls in duplicate will be sent with the patients. An Ambulance car will start from the Corps Rest Station, St CREN with the cases to be conveyed to PERONNE, and will call at the Corps Rest Station, DOINGT, to pick up the cases there if there is room for them in the car or to be accompanied by another car from DOINGT if necessary. The cars will arrive at PERONNE by 9.30 A.M. They will probably be required to wait to take the cases back. Rations for the day for patients and personnel will be taken.

Mohave Indians Col. J. A.

June 1917

Army Form C. 2118.

WAR DIARY or INTELLIGENCE SUMMARY.

VOLUME XXVII

Instructions regarding War Diaries and Intelligence Summaries are contained in F. S. Regs., Part II. and the Staff Manual respectively. Title pages will be prepared in manuscript.

(Erase heading not required.)

[Header note, partially illegible:] Officers Commanding ... 1 & 2 MHOW Indian Cavalry ...

Place	Date	Hour	Summary of Events and Information	Remarks and references to Appendices
CAVAMONT 1/20 ovo Sheet 62 SE W.3 a 5.5.	1917 June 14		Horse transport received. Received fatigues. Very hot day.	
do	June (Fri) 15		Horse transport arrived. Received fatigues. Overriding line interrupted. SEO'B'A'D 1.0.7.a. Pay received received. Hot day.	
do	Sat June 16		Horse transport arrived. Received fatigues. Church parade 6.30 p.m. Hot day.	allocation of shells & tanks Copy I
do	Sun June 17		Army Cyclist received. Returned July am. Sergt. Clements returned from course of instruction for engineers. Hot day.	
do	Mon June 18		Advanced Driving Station marched to VADENCOURT by 1/20 ovo shut Co S.E R 16 & 8.5. ptoff over from 2 Sqd of Canadians E.T.O.	composition of Army Copy II. Admin ... received from ... Copy III
	Tues June 19		Hot day.	

Army Form C. 2118.

WAR DIARY
or
INTELLIGENCE SUMMARY.

Volume XXXII O.C.
104 M How / C 70

(Erase heading not required.)

Instructions regarding War Diaries and Intelligence Summaries are contained in F. S. Regs., Part II. and the Staff Manual respectively. Title pages will be prepared in manuscript.

Place	Date	Hour	Summary of Events and Information	Remarks and references to Appendices
CAULAINCOURT	Jan 6th		Horse transport reserve personnel fatigues. A.S.C. conveying carts direct to Sta. Cav Bus tram Devisory Station were BERNES at 11.00 hrs that 10 O.Rs of Tpt. Section collecting arrears of packages landed JANBACH SEC'BAD Brigade.	
Do			Hot day.	
do	Jan 7th		Horse transport reserve personnel fatigues Sergt CARROLL M.T. returned from course of instruction Major MATTHEWS inspected A.D.S. at VADENCOURT. Later Thunder & some rain.	
do	Jan 8th		Horse transport reserve personnel fatigues - Fire at Q.M.T Shuttle had Dress XLT day.	
do	Jan 9th		Horse transport reserve personnel fatigues - Pay received Major MATTHEWS on leave to England Capt WORLEY acting as O.C. Unit section -	
do			First hot day	

Army Form C. 2118.

WAR DIARY
INTELLIGENCE SUMMARY.

Vol XXXIV p 3

(Erase heading not required.)

10 " MIT UW 1.C. + a

Instructions regarding War Diaries and Intelligence Summaries are contained in F.S. Regs., Part II. and the Staff Manual respectively. Title pages will be prepared in manuscript.

Place	Date	Hour	Summary of Events and Information	Remarks and references to Appendices
CAVAINCOURT	June 10th		Rest	
		Dr Own	Hot day	
do	June 11th		Horse transport received Personnel fatigues - Bn reported shells unopened in	
		Ca Own	Hot day	
do	June 12		Horse transport received Personnel fatigues	
		Dr Own	Hot day	
do	June 13th		Horse transport received Personnel fatigue	
			Medical inspection all ranks	
		Dr Own	Hot day	
do	June 14th		Horse transport received Personnel fatigues	
		Ca Own	Hot day	
do	June 15th		Horse transport received Personnel fatigues	
		Ca Own	Hot day	
do	June 16th		Horse Transport received Personnel fatigues on all HT admitted sick	
			Pay received issued	
		Dr Own	Hot day	

Army Form C. 2118.

WAR DIARY
or
INTELLIGENCE SUMMARY.

Vol XXXII p 4

(Erase heading not required.)

154 M.T. of W.I.C. Jas

Place	Date	Hour	Summary of Events and Information	Remarks and references to Appendices
CAULAINCOURT	June 19th		Rest	
do	June 20		Sergt CORT alert reported from leave to England	
			one dan	
do	June 21st		Three transport received personal fatigue	
			Horse & animals dull inspection	
	Sat		one letter	
do	June 23rd		Three transport received Personal fatigue	
			One ACCIDENT reported from hospital one eye & one left shell	
			1st Class Saf. KIRTEN SINGH promoted to 2nd Class Lance Naik (Armourer)	
			from 27 (11 ?)	
			Thausser lame	
do	June 23rd		Three transport received Personal fatigue and inoculate	
			one accident wounds medical inspection	
	Calcuta		Thursday & Horsery	
	June 24th		One transport received Personal fatigue No ASP 41 reported from hospital	
			one wounded from A.D.S. 1554 A.D.S. and received at Yas EMS COST	
	Calcuta		Thursday & Horses	

2353 Wt. W3544/1454 700,000 5/15 D. D. & L. A.D.S.S./Forms/C. 2118.

Army Form C. 2118.

WAR DIARY
or
INTELLIGENCE SUMMARY. p 5 —

(Erase heading not required.)

Vol XIX

Place	Date	Hour	Summary of Events and Information	Remarks and references to Appendices
CADRINCOURT	June 21st		Horse transport arrived. Personnel following. Major MATTHEWS returned from leave to England.	
do	June 22nd		Fine day. Horse transport arrived. Personnel following. Major MATTHEWS inspected ADS at VADENCOURT.	
			Thursday.	
			Personnel arrived.	
Dalen	June 23rd		Ambulance quite full. Clinical parade 6.30pm. Cpl MEDINE (?) on leave to England.	
Dalen	June 24th		Quiet day. Horse transport arrived. Personnel following. But reception still uncertain.	
Dalen	June 25th		Fine day.	
do	June 26th		Horse transport arrived. Personnel following. Full wheelers shop.	
Dalen			Quiet day.	

Instructions regarding War Diaries and Intelligence Summaries are contained in F. S. Regs., Part II. and the Staff Manual respectively. Title pages will be prepared in manuscript.

Army Form C. 2118.

WAR DIARY

or

INTELLIGENCE SUMMARY. Vol XXXII P.6 O.C

(Erase heading not required.) 1/5th M.F.O.W. I.C.T.A.

Instructions regarding War Diaries and Intelligence
Summaries are contained in F. S. Regs., Part II.
and the Staff Manual respectively. Title pages
will be prepared in manuscript.

Place	Date	Hour	Summary of Events and Information	Remarks and references to Appendices
BEAUCOURT	June 27		Horse transport arrived. Personal fatigue. Medical inspection.	
do	"		Heavy Thunderstorm	
do	June 28		Horse transport arrived - Personal fatigue	
do	"		Rather showery day	
do	June 29		Horse transport arrived - Personnel fatigues - One relief have proceeded	
do	June 30		Fine day -	
do	"		Horse transport arrived 20 - Personnel fatigues - Pony arrived riverside - Inoculation for the month for the month 1000 O.Rs.	
Entries			very unsatisfactory	

D. Armstrong
transport shed
Army 10th MFOW 10 TA

2353 Wt. W2544/1454 700,000 5/15 D. D. & L. A.D.S.S./Forms/C. 2118.

Appendix I

Dental Centre, TINCOURT. Two Dental Surgeons. (Nos 5 & 36 C.C.S.)

A Dental Mechanical Centre will be established in the Civil Hospital, PERONNE, under charge of Captain J.W. GRAHAM, Dental Surgeon, No. 39 C.C.S., assisted by a Dental Surgeon from one of the other Casualty Cl: Stations at TINCOURT.

Officers requiring dental treatment will only be seen by appointment at C.C. Stations, and not on the visits of Dental Surgeons to Field Ambulances. Such appointments will be made by A.Ds.M.S. concerned. The visits to Field Ambulances are to be kept exclusively for NCOs and men.

The PERONNE Centre for Mechanical Dentistry will be opened during the first 10 days of June: exact date will be notified later.

This Centre has been established for:-

(a) The repair and manufacture of dentures
(b) Any special work that cannot be undertaken successfully by the Dental Surgeons, attached to C.C. Stations; especially work of a mechanical nature.

This Centre will be available both for officers and other Ranks.

Appendix III

All officers, N.C.Os. and men reporting as:—

"(a) Suffering from "shell shock";
"(b) Suffering from "Gas"
"(c) Suffering from nervous breakdown, inability to stand shell fire, or neurasthenia", will be sent to No: 41 Stationary Hospital and will not be evacuated to the Base unless:—

(I) In the case of (a), there are definite lesions and symptoms which justify the classification of the case as a battle casualty.

(II) In the case of (b), it is proved that the patient has been gassed.

Cases coming under (a) and (b) will not be returned as battle casualties in casualty reports until they have been diagnosed at No: 41 Stationary Hospital.

Cases coming under (c) will not be returned as battle casualties, but will be dealt with under instructions which are being issued by the D.M.S., Fourth Army.

Appendix II

Advanced Dressing Section
Personnel
10H MHOW / CFA

Officers

Capt N. MATTHEWS
" J. A. MACLEAN

Horse Holders

Dr ENNIS

Motor Cyclist	Pte CHILLCOTT
S.A.S.	ALLAH DITTA
W.O.	MIAN MOHAMAD
L/Cpl	LETHBY
Ward servant	TENI RAM
do	DULI CHAND
Cook	GOBIND
Sweeper	SOORTHA
do	NAND
Syce	INDAR SINGH
do	GHIBA
Bearers	29

Equipment

Fracture Box	1	Directing Poles	2
Medical Comfort Box	1	Directing Board	1
Surgical Panniers 1 & 2 No: 2		Lamps Camp	2
Trestles pair	1	Water Bottle	1
Primus Stove	1	Spare parts for wheeled Stretchers bag 1	1
Kajawa Box	1		
Cooking pots British	1	Limber wagon	1
— do — Indian	1	Water Cart	1
Fd: Medl: Companion	2	L.H. Ambulances	3
Fd: Service Haversacks	3	Thomas Sprayer in box	1
Water testing box	1	Tarpaulins	4
Splinting notes	2	Blankets	70
Stretchers	16		
Shovel	1		
Pick	1		
Axe	1		
Smoke Helmets	60		

COMMITTEE FOR THE
MEDICAL HISTORY OF THE WAR
Date 16 OCT. 1917

"Medical." Serial No: 199.

Mhow Indian Cavalry Field Ambulance.

From 1st to 31st July 1917.

Correspondence received

General's Base Office.

oOooo----

　　　　　　　　　　Date_____

	Case on which letter will be found		Initial of ⟨illegible⟩
	Main Head:	No.	

Army Form C. 2118.

WAR DIARY
or
INTELLIGENCE SUMMARY.
(Erase heading not required.)

104 M/ford A.S. in Cavalry Field Ambulance

Volume XXXIII

Instructions regarding War Diaries and Intelligence Summaries are contained in F. S. Regs., Part II. and the Staff Manual respectively. Title pages will be prepared in manuscript.

Place	Date	Hour	Summary of Events and Information	Remarks and references to Appendices
CAULAINCOURT	1917 July 1st		Horse transport paraded. Sunday day.	
do	July 2nd		Horse transport exercise. General fatigues. Bn. Serjeant drill & inspection. Capt MORLEY came on leave to England. One eye returned from hospital.	
do	July 3rd		Showery day.	
do	July 4th		Horse transport exercise. General fatigues. Col ADEY on leave in France.	
do	July 5th		Quiet day.	
do	July 6th		Horse transport exercise. General fatigues. Medical inspection. Quiet day.	
do	July 7th		Horse transport exercise. General fatigues. On. Reeve returned from hospital. A.T.D took ground from 12 noon. Quiet day.	
do	July 8th		Horse transport exercise. General fatigues. About 20 H.E. shells fell in vicinity of ambulance. No casualties or damage. Remained in R 3 risk. Quiet day.	

WAR DIARY
INTELLIGENCE SUMMARY.

Army Form C. 2118.

Vol XXXIV

10 L
O/C
104 M/tow/CZ9

Place	Date	Hour	Summary of Events and Information	Remarks and references to Appendices
CAULAINCOURT TO TERRY	July 7th		Tent return moved under orders of G.O.C. in B4th Bde to TERRY (previously W.2.C.9). Col McKINLEY reported from leave to England. Received knapsacks No 1. One mule received. Pay received.	
	On Quer		Fine day.	
TERRY	July 8th	Dy Orr	Rest. Sick receiving list. Fine day.	
do	July 9th	9 am	Horse transport exercise. Personal fatigues. Personal fatigues - sick receiving BOR3 10 R1. Fine day.	
do	July 10th		Horse transport exercise. Personal fatigues. A.D.S. handed over to A.D.S. 57/104. 2 T.A. 27 9 am reported headquarters at noon. Sick receiving BOR 9 10.R.I. Fine day.	
do	July 11th		Horse transport exercise. Personal fatigues. Bon Ingenieur child inspection. Medical inspection 6 p.m. not receiving BO.R.) 10 R1. Pay received. Fine day.	

WAR DIARY
INTELLIGENCE SUMMARY.

Vol XXXIII   P 3

Army Form C. 2118.

COY MAHON I.C. 7.a.

Place	Date	Hour	Summary of Events and Information	Remarks and references to Appendices
TERTRY	July 12th		Orders received for two days march to neighbourhood of ST P... Supt CORT Ass'nt Campbell supervising to Corps Sect renewing B.O.R. 4. 1. O.R. 2.	Copy I forwarded by dispatch rider
	Dawn		Fine day	
CARTIGNY	July 13th		Marched from TERTRY 3.0 pm arrived CARTIGNY 4.30 pm Sect renewing N.I. Motor ambulance placed under Division	Rivett Norwich app. 7000 AMIENS
	Sexton		Thunder day	
SUZANNE	July 14th		Marched from CARTIGNY at 7.30 am arrived SUZANNE 12.30 pm Sick renewing N.I.	
	Dawn		Showery day	
MORLANCOURT	July 15th		Marched from SUZANNE at 8 am arrived MORLANCOURT 1 pm Sick renewing N.I.	Mango 1/1 ORO LENS
	Dawn		Showery day	
MARIEUX	July 16th		Marched from MORLANCOURT 8.45 am arrived MARIEUX 1.0 pm Sect renewing N.I.	
	Dawn		Wet day	

Army Form C. 2118.

WAR DIARY
INTELLIGENCE SUMMARY.

(Erase heading not required.)

Instructions regarding War Diaries and Intelligence Summaries are contained in F. S. Regs., Part II. and the Staff Manual respectively. Title pages will be prepared in manuscript.

Vol XXX (1)

p 4 &
10-4 M/OW/10/a

Place	Date	Hour	Summary of Events and Information	Remarks and references to Appendices
ST MICHEL	July 17th		Marched from MARIEUX 5.45 am arrived in billets at ST MICHEL 2 pm. Rest section stayed for week. Draft from AMBALA & SEC'BAD trispahs. Capt WORLEY & Cpl ADEY reported from leave. Lt WILKINSON left on leave. All ticked sick to No 12 Stationary Hospital S.E Pit except Driver G. No 6 Stationary Hospital PREVENT Lilian N.S. Driver UNSWORTH POS at PERONNE except Driver Cowie which go by Ambulance train to LATHORE 1.G. Hospital ROUEN. Sick remaining N.l.	
do	July 18th		Horses transported received. Personnel fatigue & leave granted for temporary duty. Sick remaining Nil.	
			Decem, Slaves, day	
do	July 19th		Horse transport received. Personnel fatigue. Capt also beau from Leave. Lt R. receiving BUR 4 / O/P 6.	
			Lusin Slaves, day	
do	July 20th		Horse transport received. Several Personnel fatigue. One trooper admitted with One & M T personnel from base stationary BO PQ 1 O/P 3. Quiet day.	

2353 Wt. W2344/1454 700,000 5/15 D. D. & L. A.D.S.S./Forms/C. 2118.

Army Form C. 2118.

Instructions regarding War Diaries and Intelligence
Summaries are contained in F. S. Regs., Part II.
and the Staff Manual respectively. Title pages
will be prepared in manuscript.

WAR DIARY
or
INTELLIGENCE SUMMARY.

Vol XXXIII   p 5   OC
                   15th M TOW 1 C ?a.

(Erase heading not required.)

Place	Date	Hour	Summary of Events and Information	Remarks and references to Appendices
ST MICHEL	July 21st		Horse transport received Personal fatigue. Those Horse posted for duty with 7 4th DN. Rein. & 7th D.G.s. Pay received Parade & Well swimming. BOR 9 1075 3.	
do	July 22nd		Rest day. Horse transport paying. Church Parade 6.30 pm Lect swimming BOR 7 1075 3.	
do	July 23rd		Rest day. Horse transport received. C&B cinque drill 3 pm Box repairs drill tunicakin 6 pm. Message repaid from hospital Sgt FERRER Dn HUMBER & Pte DAVIES m. Lieut England S&P swimming BOR 9 1075 3.	
do	July 24th		Rest day. Horse transport received. CRS stable drill 3 pm. Pte MASON Dn SOUTHWOOD. T VAN DER STEEN on leave to England. Pte Runaway BOR 8 1075 3. R. WD IMHOME & DS now posted S.C. corps. Rest day.	

WAR DIARY or INTELLIGENCE SUMMARY

Army Form C. 2118.

Instructions regarding War Diaries and Intelligence Summaries are contained in F. S. Regs., Part II. and the Staff Manual respectively. Title pages will be prepared in manuscript.

Vol XXXIII

(Erase heading not required.)

Place	Date	Hour	Summary of Events and Information	Remarks and references to Appendices
ST MICHEL	July 25th		The corps elected 6730 company dull, kicked repeated tpts. Self renaming BOR 9 1 OR 2.	
do	" 26th	Du Cen	Fine day	
			Two transport drivers took recurring POR 9 1 OR 2.	
do	July 27th	Green Fri day	Fine transport drivers kepudin for[?] and in infantry[?] equ'd. T Mr Silver	
			C.B.O. Statsler dull shew t of incoming POR 9 1 OR 3 -	
do	July 28th	Du find	Fine day -	
do	July 29th		Three transport drivers and 1 and 6 minubalium after Span day received recruit half incoming BOR 9 1 OR 9 -	
		Ca Cen	Fine day	
do	July 30th		Ruet statements 18 OR 9 1 OR K -	
		Cken	Heavy Thunderstorms.	
do	July 30th		Find transport received - C.B.O. Statsler dull heal incoming Section paraded for self tuning 31 R 9 1 OR 6 -	
		Da Cen	showery day	

Army Form C. 2118.

WAR DIARY
or
INTELLIGENCE SUMMARY.

(Erase heading not required.)

Instructions regarding War Diaries and Intelligence Summaries are contained in F.S. Regs., Part II. and the Staff Manual respectively. Title pages will be prepared in manuscript.

Vol XXVII

Place	Date	Hour	Summary of Events and Information	Remarks and references to Appendices
ST ROCH	July 31st		Have to report arrival of 2/4th Company dull & instruction in first aid was carried out. B.O.R. 1076 for day. Instruction for the wounded T.A.B. 100.75 —	

I. Anderton
Major but
Captain Commanding 1/74

Appendix I

(1) The Division will move northwards between July 13th and 18th.

(2) Cavalry Fd. Ambulances will march and billet under the orders of G.O.C. the Brigade to which they are now attached.

(3) Motor Ambulances are at disposal of Officers Commanding, Cav. Fd. Ambulances, who will so arrange their moves as to prevent interference with troops on the line of march.

(4) The Divl. Sanitary Section will move under orders to be issued separately to Officer Commanding

(5) Endeavour will be made to restrict evacuation of sick on the line of march as far as possible. When necessary British sick will be evacuated to the nearest Medical Unit, Indian sick to the LUCKNOW CCS. at PERONNE-LA-CHAPELETTE until a section of that unit has been established in the area into which the Division is moving. All cases admitted to a Field Ambulance of another Formation will be shown as transferred. Cases admitted to a C.C. Station will be shown as evacuated. A list of certain Medical Units on the line of march is as under:-

CAPPY-SUZANNE area	No. 38 CCS BRAY
RIBEMONT-HEILLY "	No. 56 CCS DERNANCOURT
ORVILLE, SARTON, AUTHIE "	No. 3 Canad. Staty. Hospital DOULLENS
HOUVIN-ETREE-WAMIN "	No. 6 Stationary Hospl FREVENT
GAUCHIN-ST. POL "	No. 12 " " ST. POL.

(6) A.F.W. 3185 will be despatched in time to reach this Office by noon daily without fail.

(7) On arrival at final destination SEC'D CFA will remain closed but will collect sick from its own Brigade area, MHOW CFA will open for reception of British and Indian sick of AMBALA and SEC'BAD Brigades. Site will be indicated on arrival of this unit. CANADIAN CFA will open for reception of sick from CANADIAN CAV. Brigade.

COMMITTEE FOR THE
MEDICAL HISTORY OF THE WAR
Date 16 OCT 1917

"Medical." Serial No: 199.

Mhow Cavalry Field Ambulance.

From 1st to 31st August, 1917.

Army Form C. 2118.

WAR DIARY
or
INTELLIGENCE SUMMARY.
(Erase heading not required.)

VOLUME XXXIV

10 4 M&OW Field an Cavalry Field Ambulance O-C

Place	Date	Hour	Summary of Events and Information	Remarks and references to Appendices
	1917			
ST MICHEL	August 1st		Horse transport exercise. Pack Saddle Section paraded for inspection by DDMS Cavalry Corps 10 am. Medical Inspection 6 pm.	
do	2nd	Down yetter	Pte Beara A.B.C. reported for Hospital. Sick remaining B O R 7 I O R 8.	
do			Horse transport exercise A.B.C. first aid demonstration	
do			Cpl Dowie & Dr RAMSLEY on leave. Sick remaining B O R 5 I O R 10	
do	3rd	Special welfare	Horse transport exercise at 8-0 Stretcher drill.	
do			Dr HOMBER reported from leave. Sick remaining B O R 5 I O R 5.	
do		Sudden shower day		
do	4th		Horse transport exercise. A.B.C. first aid demonstration.	
			Sgt LEDGER Pte DAVIES & MARSON reported from leave.	
			Pay received received. Sick remaining B O R 7 I O R 6.	
		Shower day		
do	5th		Rest.	
do			Dr SOUTHWARD VANDER STEEN & WILKINSON returned from leave.	
			Sick remaining B O R 8 I O R 9.	
do			Fine day	

Army Form C. 2118.

Instructions regarding War Diaries and Intelligence
Summaries are contained in F.S. Regs., Part II.
and the Staff Manual respectively. Title pages
will be prepared in manuscript.

WAR DIARY
INTELLIGENCE SUMMARY.

Vol XXXIV

O.C. 104 M/Tow I.O.T.a.

(Erase heading not required.)

Place	Date	Hour	Summary of Events and Information	Remarks and references to Appendices
ST MICHEL	Aug 6th		Horse transport exercise. C.P.S.C. stretcher drill 3 pm. Box respirator drill inspection 6 pm Sick remaining B.O.R. 10 I.O.R. 8 one driver at d. Dentist ship.	
do	Aug 7th		Horse transport exercise. A.T.S. Company drill 3 pm Capt MATTHEWS & Lieut MURDOCH & Capt COMERFORD on leave. Sick remaining B.O.R. 9. I.O.R. 8 Snowy day.	
do	Aug 8th		Horse transport exercise. Medical inspection 6 pm. one I.O.R. 7 repaired from hospital. Sick remaining B.O.R. 10. I.O.R. 9. Snowy day.	
do	Aug 9th		Horse transport exercise. Personal fatigues. Pay received. Sick remaining B.O.R.) I.O.R. 9 Snowy day.	
do	Aug 10th		Horse transport exercise. Personal fatigues. Sick remaining B.O.R. 9. I.O.R. 10. Snowy day.	

Army Form C. 2118.

WAR DIARY
or
INTELLIGENCE SUMMARY.
(Erase heading not required.)

Vol XXXIV   P 3
04/M/20v/.0.7.C

Instructions regarding War Diaries and Intelligence Summaries are contained in F.S. Regs., Part II and the Staff Manual respectively. Title pages will be prepared in manuscript.

Place	Date	Hour	Summary of Events and Information	Remarks and references to Appendices
ST MIHIEL	Aug 11th	Dawn	Horse transport service. Personal fatigues. Sick revised BOR 9. IOR 10. Showery day.	
do	Aug 12th	later	Rest. Sick revised BOR 8. IOR 11. Showery day.	
do	Aug 13	Dawn	Horse transport service. Personal fatigues. Sick revised BOR 8. IOR 11. Showery day.	
do	Aug 14th	snow	Horse transport service. Personal fatigues. Sick remaining BOR 6. IOR 9. Showery day.	
do	Aug 15th	snow	Survival threshers. Sick remaining BOR 6. IOR 10. Showery day.	
do	Aug 16th	later	Horse transport service. Personal fatigues. Sick revised BOR 11. IOR 5. Medical inspection. Showery day.	

Army Form C. 2118.

WAR DIARY
or
INTELLIGENCE SUMMARY.

Vol XXIV   p 4   1st MIT[ory] / C [Sec]

Instructions regarding War Diaries and Intelligence Summaries are contained in F. S. Regs. Part II. and the Staff Manual respectively. Title pages will be prepared in manuscript.

(Erase heading not required.)

Place	Date	Hour	Summary of Events and Information	Remarks and references to Appendices
ST MICHEL	Aug 17th Daley		Horse transport exercise. Pack saddles paraded. Sick running BORS 1 OR 5	
do	Aug 18th		Showery day. Horse transport exercised - also first aid demonstration. Sick running (BOR) 1 OR 5 Pay received/issued Capt MATTHEWS reported from leave	
do	Aug 19th Daley		Showery day Church parade 5.30pm 5 OR's leave joined from base. The 4th H.T. drivers reck	
do	Aug 20th Daley		Fine day Horse transport exercise. Bn inspection still in progress. Sick running BOR 5. 1.O.1. OR 4.	
do	Aug 21st Daley		Fine day Inspection of A Echelon with Am Bar A Beh by MGO 5th Cav Div. Also first aid demonstration. Capt MATTHEWS on company lets in Bn offices of the division. Sick running BOR 5.1 O 1. 1 OR 7	
	Daley		Fine day	

Army Form C. 2118.

WAR DIARY
or
INTELLIGENCE SUMMARY.
(Erase heading not required.)

Vol XXIV

Instructions regarding War Diaries and Intelligence Summaries are contained in F.S. Regs., Part II. and the Staff Manual respectively. Title pages will be prepared in manuscript.

Place	Date	Hour	Summary of Events and Information	Remarks and references to Appendices
ST MICHEL	Aug 22nd		Horse transport exercise - arse stretcher drill - Medical inspection. Self remaining BOR 6. 1.0.1. 1.OR 4. 2/NS B441 in leave to Ingland. On sergeant 2/0/17 admitted sick. On time A/C #7. discharged h'duty.	
		Calm Showery day		
do	Aug 23rd		Horse transport exercise. Self remaining BOR 6. 1.0.1. 1.OR 4.	
		Calm Showery day—		
do	Aug 24th		Horse transport exercise - arse stretcher drill - Medical inspection. Self remaining B.OR 6. 1.OR 10.	
		Calm Showery day		
do	Aug 25th		Horse transport exercise - ARQ Company drill. Self remaining BOR 9. 1.OR 3. Pay received received.	
		Calm Showery day— Rch		
do	Aug 26th		Self remaining BOR 9 1.OR 7—	
		Calm Showery day		

Army Form C. 2118.

WAR DIARY
INTELLIGENCE SUMMARY.
(Erase heading not required.)

Vol XXIV p 6. O.C.
104 M.T.C.W. 1.C.T.A.

Place	Date	Hour	Summary of Events and Information	Remarks and references to Appendices
ST MICHEL	Aug 27th		Three transport exercise. Stock receiving Box 7. I.C.T. 8. Box repairs inspection by D.A.D. for N.C.O. Even showery day.	
do	Aug 28th		Three transport exercise. Stock receiving Box 7. I.C.T. 9. Heavy gale.	
do	Aug 29th		Three transport exercise. Stock receiving Box 6. I.C.T. 7. Two of I.C.T. 7 admitted sick.	
do	Aug 30th		Three transport exercise. Stock receiving Box 9. I.C.T. 7. On C.T. 7 admitted sick. On riding horse received from Do'bril I.C.T.	
do	Aug 31st		Three transport exercise. Stock receiving Box 11. I.C.T. 8. Very showery day.	

E. Alcock Lieut
Major? R.M.C.

Comdt / 104 M.T.C.W./C.T.A.

164. (Anton) Fd. Res. F.O.

COMMITTEE FOR THE
MEDICAL HISTORY OF THE WAR
Date 12 DEC. 1917

"Medical"

Serial No. 199.
Army Form C. 2118.

WAR DIARY
or
INTELLIGENCE SUMMARY.

Officer Commanding
104 Mhow Indian Cavalry Field Ambulance

Volume XXXV

(Erase heading not required.)

Place	Date	Hour	Summary of Events and Information	Remarks and references to Appendices
	1917			
ST MICHEL	Sept 1st		Env. Corps three shows. Taking sick from AMBALA Cav Bde only.— Sick remaining B.O.R. 11. I.O.R. 8.	
do	Sept 2nd		Wet day. Church parade 5.30pm.	
do			Capt V MATHEWS RAMC Dental revaccinated sick. One NCO admitted sick. Sick remaining B.O.R. 10 I.O.R. 8	
do	Sept 3rd		Showery day. Horse transport received. Ply went hill by hand walk. Am Wagons did inspection. One NCO admitted sick. Sick remaining B.O.R. 9 I.O.R. 8	
do			Showery day.— Three transport received — taken round Company drill.— NCO remaining B.O.R. 5 I.O.R. 10	
do			Showery day.—	
do	Sept 5th		Horse transport exercised afield stables drill indeed inspection. Sick remaining B.O.R. 5 I.O.R. 9.—	
do			Showery day.—	

Army Form C. 2118.

WAR DIARY
or
INTELLIGENCE SUMMARY.
(Erase heading not required.)

Volume XXXV

Officers Commanding
104 M How Bn. Canty R.G.A. [?]

Instructions regarding War Diaries and Intelligence
Summaries are contained in F.S. Regs., Part II.
and the Staff Manual respectively. Title pages
will be prepared in manuscript.

Place	Date	Hour	Summary of Events and Information	Remarks and references to Appendices
St Michel	Sept 6th		Horse transport exercise. Sgt Ledger returned from hospital. Sick remained B.O.R. 5 I.O.R. 13.	
do	Sept 7th		Fine hot day. Horse transport exercise. Indian rank & file paraded. B.O.R. remaining B.O.R. 5 I.O.R. 10.	
do	Sept 8th		Fine day. Horse transport exercise. Pay sheets - 2nd parade. Pay received Rec'd Bn Remaining B.O.R. 5 I.O.R. 10.	
do	Sept 9th		Delivery day. Hot day. Horse transport exercise on case returned from hospital. Sick remaining B.O.R. 5 I.O.R. 9.	
do	Sept 10th		Calm fine day. Horse transport exercise. Indian rank & file real drill. Bn inspected and inspection sick remaining B.O.R. 5 I.O.R. 6.	
do	Sept 11th		Horse transport exercise. Indian rank & file real drill sick remaining B.O.R. 10 I.O.R. 10. Recovery day.	

Army Form C. 2118.

WAR DIARY
or
INTELLIGENCE SUMMARY.
(Erase heading not required.)

Vol XXXV   p.3   O.C.
104 M HOW /C/7a.

Place	Date	Hour	Summary of Events and Information	Remarks and references to Appendices
ST MELOIR	Sept 11th		Horse transport exercise. Indian rank, physical drill - medical inspection. Still remaining BOR 8 / OR 7.	
do	Calam Sept 12th		Fine day —	
	Sept 13th		Horse transport exercise Indian rank, physical drill. Lt Kenny rejoining BOR 11/OR 6. One OR rejoined from hospital. One rank received from base.	
	Calam		Pay received — Fine day —	
do	Sept 14th		Horse transport exercise Indian rank, physical drill. Lt Kenny rejoining BOR 14/OR 8. One OR admitted hospital. Capt Rev A SELWYN on leave.	
	Calam		Fine day — Rest	
do	Sept 15th		Horse transport exercise Indian rank, physical drill. Sick remaining BOR 14/OR 10.	
	Calam Sept 16th		Fine day — One AS.C H.T. rejoined from hospital. Still remaining BOR 14/OR 10.	
	Calam		Fine day —	

2353 Wt. W2544/1454 700,000 5/15 D. D. & L. A.D.S.S./Forms/C. 2118.

Army Form C. 2118.

WAR DIARY
or
INTELLIGENCE SUMMARY.

(Erase heading not required.)

Instructions regarding War Diaries and Intelligence Summaries are contained in F.S. Regs., Part II. and the Staff Manual respectively. Title pages will be prepared in manuscript.

Vol XXXV   10th I.C.D.

Place	Date	Hour	Summary of Events and Information	Remarks and references to Appendices
ST MICHEL	Sept 17th		Horse transport received Indian troops, physical drill. Bn to sprinkler shed inspection. Sick remaining BoR 10 IOR 12.	
do			Labour fine day	
do	Sept 18th		Horse transport received Indian troops, physical drill. Sick remaining BoR 11 IOR 12	
do			Labour fine day	
do	Sept 19th		Horse transport service. Indian ranks physical drill. Sick remaining BoR 9 IOR 12	
			Major MATTHEWS on leave. Medical inspection	
do			Labour fine day	
do	Sept 20th		Horse transport received. Sick remaining BoR 8 IOR 12. Pay received missing	
do			Labour fine day	
do	Sept 21st		Horse transport service. Sick remaining BoR 9 I OR 10.	
do			Labour fine day	
do	Sept 22nd		Pack section parade. All ranks paraded for preceding through gas chamber.	
			Sick remaining BoR 8 I OR 10	
			Horse transport service	
do			Labour fine day	

Army Form C. 2118.

WAR DIARY
or
INTELLIGENCE SUMMARY.

Vol XXX   p 5.   DC
10th M How 10 7 a

(Erase heading not required.)

Instructions regarding War Diaries and Intelligence Summaries are contained in F. S. Regs., Part II and the Staff Manual respectively. Title pages will be prepared in manuscript.

Place	Date	Hour	Summary of Events and Information	Remarks and references to Appendices
ST MICHEL	Sept 23rd		Still remained. BoR 8 1oR 8.	
			Taceen. Fine day.	
do	Sept 24		Horse transport exercise. Indian rank route march.	
			Still remaining. BoR 7 1oR 10. Capt MacLean on leave.	
			Caeen. Fine day.	
do	Sept 25th		Horse transport exercise. Indian rank route march. Post letters found.	
			Still remaining. BoR 11 1oR 8. 2 stray horses arrested.	
			Taceen. Fine day.	
do	Sept 26th		Inspection by S.D.M.L. Cav Corps. Medical inspection.	
			Still remaining. BoR. 10 1oR. 10.	
			Taceen. Fine day.	
do	Sept 27th		Horse transport exercise. Pay received. Still remaining. BoR 9 1oR 8.	
			Caeen. Fine day.	
do	Sept 28th		Horse transport exercise. Preceived fatigue.	
			Still remaining. BoR. 10 1oR. 9.	
			Taceen. Fine day.	

2353 Wt. W2544/1454 700,000 5/15 D. D. & L.   A.D.S.S./Forms/C. 2118.

Army Form C. 2118.

WAR DIARY
~~INTELLIGENCE SUMMARY.~~

(Erase heading not required.)

Place	Date	Hour	Summary of Events and Information	Remarks and references to Appendices
ST MICHEL	Sept 29th		Huns transport services Indian trucks with wound. Still remaining ROR. 10. 10R.9	
Solerin			Fine day	
	Sept 30th		Church parade 6 p.m. Still remaining ROR.15. 10R.11. Major MATTHEWS returned from Capt WORLEY on leave.	
Solerin			Fine day	

Lieutenant
Map ref.
C in Sp 104 MHow 1.C.9.a.

COMMITTEE FOR THE
MEDICAL HISTORY OF THE WAR
Date -8 FEB. 1918

Army Form C.2118.

General Medical 199

WAR DIARY
or
INTELLIGENCE SUMMARY.
(Erase heading not required.)

VOLUME XXXVI

1st Officier Commanding
104 M How Brigade Canadian Field Artillery

Instructions regarding War Diaries and Intelligence Summaries are contained in F.S. Regs., Part II. and the Staff Manual respectively. Title pages will be prepared in manuscript.

Place	Date	Hour	Summary of Events and Information	Remarks and references to Appendices
ST MICHEL	1917 Oct 1st		Horse transport exercise. Personal fatigues. One case admitted sick. Sick remaining ROR 11 I.O.R. 12.	
do	Oct 2nd		Fine day. Inspection by G.O.C 5th Cav Div. Bn reprinted in inspection. Sick remaining ROR 13 I.O.R 11.	
do	Oct 3rd		Fine day. Horse transport exercise. Indoor work, physical drill. One a/c/c H.T. posted for duty. Sick remaining ROR 9 I.O.R 10. Medical inspection.	
do	Oct 4th		Fine day. Horse transport exercise. Personal fatigues. Sick remaining ROR 6 I.O.R 8. Henry Thomson.	
do	Oct 5th		Horse transport exercise. Pack section parade. Indoor work, physical drill. Cpl SHEPHERD on leave. Sick remaining ROR 9 I.O.R 8. Orders received to march next early on 7 to west.	
do	Oct 6th		Fine day. Horse transport exercise. Personal fatigues.	

Army Form C. 2118.

WAR DIARY
or
INTELLIGENCE SUMMARY

(Erase heading not required.)

Vol XXX   104 M / OW / a 2 L

Place	Date	Hour	Summary of Events and Information	Remarks and references to Appendices
ST MICHEL	Oct 6th	early	Capt MACLEAN R.A.M.C. returned from leave. Cpl FIRTH R.A.M.C. proceeded from St Omer Supply Column on return from leave. Sick remaining B.O.R. 1. O.R. 1. Orders received to march in N.E. northwards to THIENNES area (M.109,000) HAZEBROUCK	
THIENNES	Oct 7th	later	Ambulance marched at 6.20 to THIENNES. Arrived 2.30 pm. Orders received to stand fast next day. Sick remaining B.O.R. 1 O.R.1.	App I orders for movement of unit Bn.
		later	Wet day.	
do	Oct 8th		Horse transport exercised. Personnel fatigues. Sick remaining B.O.R. 1 O.R. 1.	
		later	Fine day.	
do	Oct 9th		Horse transport exercised. Personnel fatigues. Well numbering B.O.R. 1 O.R.1. Sgt SHEPHERD R.A.M.C. proceeded on leave, Acting Sergeant.	App II orders for conveyance of patients.
		later	Showery day.	
do	Oct 10th		Horse transport exercised. Personnel fatigues. Well numbering B.O.R. 1 O.R.1. Orders received to endeavour march northwards tomorrow to the WATOU area.	App III Orders re reservation
		later	Showery day.	

2353 Wt. W2544/1454 700,000 5/15 D, D, & L.   A.D.S.S./Forms/C. 2118.

Army Form C. 2118.

WAR DIARY
or
INTELLIGENCE SUMMARY.

(Erase heading not required.)

Vol XXXVI p 3

104 M/70 W 1.0.7.2.

Place	Date	Hour	Summary of Events and Information	Remarks and references to Appendices
K16 d 9.8. 1/40,000 Sheet 7	Oct 11th	11 am	Ambulance marched at 9 am & arrived in WATOU area & went into camp at 3.30 p.m. Sick remaining B.O.R 1, O.R.1. Tent section opened for recp of AMBALA Fd. Ambce.	
do	Oct 12th		Free day -	
			Horse transport exercise. Personnel fatigues. Sick remaining B.O.R 2, O.R.1. Capt J. MACLEAN R.A.M.C left for 3rd Can. Div. Capt. F.R. HASSHE 23 M.E.R.A.M.C	
			joined for duty	
			Pay received remand.	
			Showery day.	
do	Oct 13th	Dawn	Horse transport exercise. Personnel fatigues. Sick remaining B.O.R 2, O.R.1.	
			One O.R. H.T. admitted evacuated sick.	
			Orders received to march S.W. next morning.	
		Dawn	Very wet day.	
BANDERINGHEM	Oct 14th	9 am	Ambulance marched at 9 am & arrived BANDERINGHEM 3.15 pm. Sick remaining B.O.R 1, O.R 1.	App IV Orders of Evacuation
		Dawn	Free day.	

Army Form C. 2118.

WAR DIARY
or
INTELLIGENCE SUMMARY.

(Erase heading not required.)

Instructions regarding War Diaries and Intelligence Summaries are contained in F.S. Regs., Part II and the Staff Manual respectively. Title pages will be prepared in manuscript.

Vol XXVI   No 4   104 No. 1701 / C.S.

Place	Date	Hour	Summary of Events and Information	Remarks and references to Appendices
WILLIAMETZ	Oct 15th		Ambulance marched to 0.45 am reached WILLIAMETZ 2 am. Sick receiving BOR 2/OR1. 1 notify here received from leave.	App I Orders in evacuation
		Noon	Fine day.	
CONTES 1/100,000 ABBEVILLE Sheet 14	Oct 16th		Ambulance marched at 8.45 am reached CONTES 2.30 pm Sick receiving BOR 3/OR1. Tent section opened for reception. Sick receiving BOR 3/OR1.	
		Dawn	Fine day.	
do	Oct 17th		Three transport exercise. Received fatigues. Sick receiving BOR 6/OR2.	
		Noon	Fine day.	
do	Oct 18th		Three transport exercise. Capt WORLEY R.A.M.C. joined from leave. 1. Rank orderly. 1 waiter orderly. 2 ARB left for duty. BOR 6/OR4 Sick receiving - BOR 6/OR4. One A.S.C. H.T. rejoined from C.C.S. with 32 Cas Posed BAffs.	
			Fine day.	
do	Oct 19th		Three transport exercise. Received fatigues. Sick receiving BOR 4/OR1. Pay received. Received Capt FIRTH R.A.M.C. on temporary duty with 20 Fd amb.	
			Fine day.	

WAR DIARY

INTELLIGENCE SUMMARY

Army Form C. 2118.

Instructions regarding War Diaries and Intelligence Summaries are contained in F.S. Regs., Part II. and the Staff Manual respectively. Title pages will be prepared in manuscript.

Vol XXXVI

Place	Date	Hour	Summary of Events and Information	Remarks and references to Appendices
CONTES	Oct 2	—	Three transport recovered. Personnel fatigues. Rd inspection. Dental parade. Two 2/4/ VT mules	104 M/ HOW 1078
			Rank & R. joined for duty. Sgt HUGHES reported from 447 Co. Ord Reinforcements	
			transferred to 9 H.Q. Sepoy RIDDEN SINGH reported from dismounted temporary arrangement	
			Sick remaining ROR 6 IOR 2.	
do	Oct 3 AM		One bar.	
			Church parade. Rd inspection. Indian ranks bath. Sick remaining BOR 10 IOR 4.	
do	Oct 4 PM		Fine day.	
			Three transport received. Personnel fatigues. Rd inspection. Sick remaining	
to		AM	Sick remaining BOR 11 IOR 4.	
do	Oct 5 PM		Showery day.	
			Three transport received. Personnel fatigues. Sick remaining BOR 8 IOR 4.	
do	Oct 6	AM	Showery day.	
			Three transport received. Personnel fatigues. Sick remaining BOR 9 IOR 4.	
		PM	Showery day. Medical inspection.	
do	Oct 7		Three transport received. Personnel fatigues. Sick remaining BOR 8 IOR 2.	
			Heavy rain reported in evening. 1 hour showery day.	
			Cols	

Army Form C. 2118.

WAR DIARY
or
INTELLIGENCE SUMMARY.

(Erase heading not required.)

Instructions regarding War Diaries and Intelligence Summaries are contained in F. S. Regs., Part II. and the Staff Manual respectively. Title pages will be prepared in manuscript.

Place	Date	Hour	Summary of Events and Information	Remarks and references to Appendices
CONTES	Oct 26th		Transport carried. Received fatigues for trenches. Received R.R.Q. 10/26. Pay received recruit marching exercises, repairs to dug outs &c.	
"	Oct 27th		Calm showery day. Transport received. Received fatigues. Stokes running Bdec 10/26. Armies day.	
"	Oct 28th		Calm showery day. Transport received. Received fatigues. Received R.R.Q. 10/26.	
			Inspection.	
			Rainy Windy day.	
"	Oct 29th		Transport received. Received fatigues. Rec. running B.O. 10/26.	
			Repairs to dug outs inspection	
			Fine Showery day.	
"	Oct 30th		Transport received. Received fatigues. Rec. running R.R.Q. 10/26.	
			Calm fine day.	
"	Oct 31st		Transport received. Received fatigues. Still running R.R.Q. 10/26.	
			Inspection of hospital by BGC Can. Corps	
			Fine day	

[signatures]

Appendix I

Following are medical arrangements on arriving in Second Army Area, they will come into force from noon October 4th:—

British Sick will be evacuated to whichever of the 4 C.C. Stations at REMY siding is receiving. These are:— No. 10 & No. 17 British No. 2 & No. 3 Canadian. Indian Sick to No. 2 C.C.S. at OULEASTEENE near (BAILLEUL) for the present.

(2) Each Fd. Amb: will collect sick of its own Brigade and of any unit of Divi: Troops in its locality.

(3) A & D. Books will be kept and Daily States will be rendered in time to reach this office by noon.

(4) Evacuation of sick will be carried out under arrangements to be made by Units themselves. Officers Comdg: MHOW & SEC'D C.F.A's will act in communication in respect of evacuation of Indian ranks.

sd/ A.T. Macnab
Colonel Ims
ADMS 5" Cav: Div.

4-10-14

Appendix XXII.

The following location of Medical Units in this area are forwarded for information :-

A.D.M. Stores   No. 2 Canadian REMY Siding

Dental Cases :- Army C.C. Station

Ophthalmic Centres :- No. 50 C.C. Station
                       MONT-DES-CATS

Scabies :- Army Scabies Station, MONT-DES-CATS.

Mobile Lab : (Bac) NO 1 REMY Siding
             (Hyg) ST. MARIE CAPPEL

Sd/ Lt H Burney Capt RAMC
for ADMS 5" Cav: Div

8/10/17

Appendix III

O.C. MHOVV DHQ

On arrival in this area Indian sick will be evacuated to No: 3 Canadian C.C. Station at REMY siding where arrangements for their reception have now been completed.

9/10/14

Sd/ A.J. Macnab
Colonel Dmo
ADMS 5" Cav: Div.

Appendix IV

During the moves Westwards the following will be the medical arrangements:-

East of ST. OMAR British Sick will be evacuated to No. 15 CCS at EBBLINHEM on the HAZEBROUCK-ST OMER Road. West of ST. OMER, they will be sent to NEW ZEALAND Stationary Hospital at WISQUES (HAZEBROUCK Sheet 5A.C.4)

Indian Sick on 15" & 16" will be dealt with as detailed in ADMS No: 5864/17 of 9/10/17 i.e. to No. 3 Canad: CCS REMY SIDING.

You will open on arrival at destination and be prepared to take both British and Indian Sick

Orders for evacuation after 17" of Indian Sick will issue later.

Sd/ A.J. Macnab
Colonel AMS
ADMS 5" Cav: Div

14/10/17

Appendix V

The following will be the arrangements for evacuation of sick in this area:-

British to No: 59 C.C. Station at HESDIN.

Indians will be evacuated under arrangements to be notified later.

Sd/ W H B Bonney
Capt R.A.M.C.
for A.D.M.S. 5" Cav: Div

16/10/17

Appendix VI

The following will be the Medical Arrangements while in this Area:—

(1) Dental cases:— Those that cannot be dealt with by the Dental Surgeon, attached to CANAD CFA to be sent to the AID, ETAPLES, to arrive by 9.30 A.M.

(2) Eye Cases:— To No: 924 General Hospital, ETAPLES to arrive by 9.30 a.m.

(3) Officers to the D of Westminster Hospl: ETAPLES

(4) Medical Stores: from No:6 Base Depot at ETAPLES.

Sd/ W H B Binney
Capt RAMC
for ADMS 5" Cav: Div:

19/10/14

COMMITTEE FOR THE
MEDICAL HISTORY OF THE WAR
Date -8 FEB. 1918

199.

Army Form C. 2118

WAR DIARY
or
INTELLIGENCE SUMMARY.

(Erase heading not required.)

Vol. XXXVII

Officer Commanding
104 M/How Indian Cavalry Field Ambulance

Instructions regarding War Diaries and Intelligence Summaries are contained in F.S. Regs., Part II. and the Staff Manual respectively. Title pages will be prepared in manuscript.

Place	Date	Hour	Summary of Events and Information	Remarks and references to Appendices
CONTES	1917 Nov 1st		Horse transport exercise. BOR inspection worn for one hour. Sick remaining BOR 4 IOR 7 Dull day.	
do	Nov 2nd		Horse transport exercise. Sick remaining BOR 8 IOR 6. Pay received received. Dull day.	
do	Nov 3rd		Divisional route march respection by M.G.C Ambulance marched at 10am. Sick remaining BOR 8 IOR 6. Kit inspection. Dull day.	
do	Nov 4th		Church parade 5.30pm. Sick remaining BOR 8 IOR 7. Dull day.	
do	Nov 5th		Horse transport exercise, box respirator; drill inspection. Sick remaining BOR 5 IOR 7 One ACC H.T. joined from Base Hosp. Dull day.	
do	Nov 6th		Horse transport exercise. Sick remaining BOR 5 IOR 6. 76 Cottor Reeve left to duty with a draft. Dull day.	

2353 Wt. W2544/1454 700,000 5/15 D.D.&L. A.D.S.S./Forms/C. 2118.

Army Form C. 2118.

WAR DIARY
or
INTELLIGENCE SUMMARY.
(Erase heading not required.)

Vol XXXVI

Instructions regarding War Diaries and Intelligence Summaries are contained in F. S. Regs., Part II. and the Staff Manual respectively. Title pages will be prepared in manuscript.

Place	Date	Hour	Summary of Events and Information	Remarks and references to Appendices
OONTES	Nov 7th		Horse transport services. Nothing important. Chief remaining ROR 9 1346	
			Dull day	
do	Nov 8th		Orders received to march south on 9th 74 DAVIES promoted to Corporal clerk.	App I. orders for march
			Fine day	
REMAISNIL	Nov 9th		Marched at 8.20 a.m. arrived REMAISNIL 3 p.m.	
			Wet day	
BEHENCOURT	Nov 10th		Marched at 9 a.m. arrived BEHENCOURT 1.30 p.m.	
			Fog day	
SUZANNE	Nov 11th		Marched at 3.45 p.m. arrived SUZANNE 10 p.m. 1 A.S.C.M.T. evacuated sick.	
			Cold foggy day	
CARTIGNY	Nov 12th		Marched at 4 p.m. arrived CARTIGNY (ST QUENTIN 1/100,000) 10 p.m.	
			Even foggy day	
do	Nov 13th		Regt Qr SAVIES reported from 5th Cav Batt'n sick remaining N.1.	
			Even foggy day	
do	Nov 14th		Horse transport services. Major MATHEWS on leave to PARIS. Not counting BOR 1104.	App II accompanying for details
			Even foggy day	

WAR DIARY
or
INTELLIGENCE SUMMARY.
(Erase heading not required.)

Army Form C. 2118.

Instructions regarding War Diaries and Intelligence Summaries are contained in F. S. Regs., Part II, and the Staff Manual respectively. Title pages will be prepared in manuscript.

Vol XXXVII P 3 OC 10th MTN / CFA

Place	Date	Hour	Summary of Events and Information	Remarks and references to Appendices
CARTIGNY	Nov 15th		Horse transport arrived. Pay received manual. Sick evacuated BOR 1. OR 2.	
do	Nov 16th	Dawn	Happy day	
			Horse transport arrived. Sick evacuated BOR 1. OR 1.	
do	Nov 17th	Dawn	Happy day.	
			Horse transport arrived. Sick evacuated BOR 2. OR 2.	
		Dusk	Happy day.	
			nil	
do	Nov 18th		Reconnaissance forward area & engineer dump. Sick evacuated.	
			Horse transport arrived. Sick evacuated Nil.	
do	Nov 19th	Dawn	Happy day.	
			Orders received to move to forward area. See Opp. III. Sick evacuated Nil.	
			Capt MATHEWS recalled reported from PARIS.	
		Dusk	Happy day.	
			Pack mounted section with OC left with AMBALA Cav Bde at 11.15 am mounted at BOIS DESSART (Sheet 57 C 7/40, no VLO at 7 am Remainder of unit left at 1/30 am arrived transp place at 10 am where we was driven which was a Ans Reserve party under Lt BHAT MOVED to VILLERS FORCH covering party.	
nr FINS	Nov 20th			

Army Form C. 2118.

WAR DIARY
INTELLIGENCE SUMMARY.
(Erase heading not required.)

V & XXVII   P 4

Place	Date	Hour	Summary of Events and Information	Remarks and references to Appendices
nr FINS	Nov 19th	early	Amb. Mob. Vet. post section went forward at 1 pm. advanced HQ at R.S.C. for the night. Standing by.	
		Dawn	Damp day.	
K 30 d 9	Nov 21st		Amb Mob Vet post section marched to K 21 central at 4.30 p.m. when marched under orders of 1st Cav Divn. to K 30 d.9. bivouacked before reaching marched by advanced dressing section with LB H41 r.12 beaver supply dep	
EQUANCOURT	Nov 22nd	Dawn	Amb. Mob. Vet. post & advanced dressing section reported 3rd Cav Div. convoy of EQUANCOURT 3 p.m. Vet. section reported next from ADMS	
ETINEHEM	Nov 23rd		Ambulance marched with Australs Mob. at 6.30 am arriving in billets at ETINEHEM 1 pm.	App IV arrangements for billets
		Dawn	Foggy day	
do	Nov 24th		Horse transport exercise. Capt H.P. Hall R.A.V.C. joined for duty	
		Dawn	Wet day	
do	Nov 25th		Rest	
			Still receiving kit	
		Dawn	Wet day	

Army Form C. 2118.

WAR DIARY
or
INTELLIGENCE SUMMARY.
(Erase heading not required.)

Vol XXXVII p 5

134 M.T.W. 1 O.T.C. O.C.

Place	Date	Hour	Summary of Events and Information	Remarks and references to Appendices
ETINEHEM	Nov 26th		Horse transport arrived. Pay received. Received Sec.Lt reinancing ROR 1/17th.	
		Evening	Mostly dry. Orders received to move east on 27th.	
TERRY	Nov 27th		Marched at 9.30 am. Arrived TERRY 3pm. Tent section open for w.k.	
		Evening	of AMBALA Pde. Still remaining Nil and Army	
do	Nov 28th		Horse transport arrived. Still remaining Nil.	
			Wet day.	
do	Nov 29th		Horse transport received. Major G.N.C. MATTHEWS on leave to PARIS	
			Capt A. COLLINS R.A.M.C. joined for duty. Still remaining ROR 1/17th 1 O.R.	
	Dec 1st		Dull day.	
	Nov 30th		Orders received at 9.30 a.m. to proceed with 16th AMBALA Pde at once. Pack section	
			moved off at 10.30 am. No operation orders. All transport, less tents & supplies and	
VILLERS FAUCON			Cross Staff under a guard, followed. Arrived VILLERS FAUCON 1 pm (Ref 57K/1/44000_.	
			Capt HASSARD joined Pde HQ. 1 Cpl COLLINS 134 Lancers. Capt WORLEY with pack returns	
			followed Pde HQ. to W.18 central arriving 4 pm. Horsed ambulances with Capt	
			Rev. SELWYN were on the road a few hundred yards west. Dressing & few casualties.	
			Pack Section moved to open battle, were cancelled almost immediately.	

Army Form C. 2118.

WAR DIARY
or
INTELLIGENCE SUMMARY.
(Erase heading not required.)

Vol XXXVII

15th MHGMT O.7.2

Instructions regarding War Diaries and Intelligence Summaries are contained in F.S. Regs., Part II. and the Staff Manual respectively. Title pages will be prepared in manuscript.

Place	Date	Hour	Summary of Events and Information	Remarks and references to Appendices
VILLERS FAUCON	14 Nov		Three Stretcher bearers sent out to an A.D.S. at HEUDICOURT — one & 9th Nov wounded evacuated by each section — when received that report would that GAUCHE Wood in the morning. Arrangements made with A.D.S. HEUDICOURT to convey them in exchange for review of two stretcher-both ambulances spowers & toning at 1 am Dec 1st	

D. Quentherst
Lieut Col
ADMS 10th Div CTS

Appendix No. I

Extract from Operation Order Medical No. 11.

Ref Map 1/100,000 sheet Jun 11   8th November 1914

1. The Division will move South on November 9th & 10th.

2. Field Ambulances will march & billet under orders of the Brigade to which they are attached.

3. Motor Ambulances will be at the disposal of Officers Commanding Cavalry Field Ambulances who will ensure that they move to their destination in such a manner as not to interfere with troops on the march.

4. Sanitary Section will move with the Supply Column.

5. Officer Commanding Canadian C.F.A. will detail an officer for Medical Charge of the Dismounted Reinforcements. He will report to O.C. Dismounted Reinforcements at NAMIN tomorrow the 9th inst. A Motor Ambulance will be placed at his disposal by the unit to which he belongs. While in this area he will evacuate British sick to No 59 C.C.S. Hesdin. Indian sick to No 6 St. Hospital FREVENT. Officer Commanding 2nd Bad 1.C.F.A., will detail a Ward orderly to assist the Medical Officer. Dismounted Reinforcements. Names of Medical Officer and Ward orderly selected will be furnished to this office forthwith.

6. Following are arrangements for evacuation of sick

OUTREBOIS Area British ranks to No 3 Canadian Sta. Hospital ~~Hesdin~~ DOULLENS.

Ref Map

OUTREBOIS Area.
    Indian Ranks to N° 6,
Stationary Hospital FREVENT

CONTAY area. British Ranks to N° 56 CCS
                                EDGEHILL.
         Indian Ranks to LUCKNOW.
     CCS at PERONNE-LA-CHAPELETTE

⚹ Reports to FRESSIN up to 11am 10th inst.
Later location of Report Centre will be
notified. Daily States to reach this office by
10-30 am daily

☩ ~~Acknowledge~~

Appendix No 2.

The following are the arrangements for evacuation of sick etc while in this area.

British
Ordinary sick to No 5 or 55 CCS at TINCOURT
Infectious cases to No 56 C.C.S. at EDGEHILL
Self-Inflicted Wounds to No 41 Sta. Hospital at GAILLY
N.Y.D.N. cases to No 41 Sta Hospital at GAILLY
Eye cases to No 3 CCS., at GREVILLERS.
Scabies cases to DOINGT

Indians will be evacuated to LUCKNOW C.C.S at PERONNE-LA-CHAPELETTE

Medical Stores will be drawn from No 14 A.D.M. Stores at TINCOURT.

Mobile Laboratories
No 16. (Bac) at PERONNE-LA-CHAPELETTE
" 22 (Hyg) at ————— " —————

SECRET

Appendix No 3

Extract from Operation Order Medical No 12

Reference Map.
1/40,000   15th November 1917

4. The Division will be ready to move forward from the FINS area at ZERO plus 2½ hours. (Zero hour 6.20 am. 20th)

5. Brigades and O.s.C Divisional Troops will arrange for guides to meet units at NURLU, and direct them to their places in the FINS area.

6. Water :— in area N.E. of FINS.

Brigade point at V.6.d.6.y.) all on East of
    "   "   " W.1.a.1.8) road from
    "   "   " Q.31.c.2.2.) FINS—METZ.

Each point is capable of watering 2,500 horses in one hour. Troughs must be used from both sides simultaneously. Fences with in + out notices will be prepared. Good policing is essential and each Brigade will send forward one officer and 6 men to superintend watering.

7. Pack Mounted Sections will move from present area to "Forward Concentration Area" with their respective Brigades.

8. Field Ambulances, less Pack Mounted Sections, + less any G.S. Wagons of Tent Division so immobelyzed will move together. Their position in column of route is indicated in Appendix "A". Canadian C.F.A. leading M.H.O.N / CFA in rear.

9. G.S. Wagons temporarily immobilized in present area will be brought up to the concentration area as soon as possible + the teams sent back for this purpose should return with the wagons not later than ZERO plus 1.

10. Heavy Sections of Cavalry Field Ambulances will remain concentrated at FINS. Medical officers in command of these Sections will be available for employment at IIIrd Main Dressing Station at V.18.c.0.7. on FINS–NURLU Rd or for assistance in evacuating the unit will move

Light Sections will move forward with No 2
'A' Echelons of Brigades.

11. A Bearer party consisting of 1 officer from M How. and Canadian Cavalry Field Ambulances and 24 other ranks from each Cavalry Field Ambulance respectively with 12 stretchers and all available wheeled carriers will be conveyed by motor ambulances to VILLERS-PLOUICH. The convoy will leave FINS at ZERO hour plus 1. From this point each party will, as soon as the three Brigades of the Division have passed, move on RUMILLY where a Divisional dressing Station and collecting post for walking wounded will be formed from which Bearer parties will be available for the collection of wounded under the orders of the officer Commanding. The motors conveying the party will be so packed at VILLERS-PLOUICH, as to avoid any interference with traffic, & will be utilised for the evacuation of casualties when circumstances permit.

12. Ambulance transport moving with No 2 Echelon will rendezvous at RUMILLY as soon as conditions allow. The motor ambulances previously left at VILLERS-PLOUICH, will be utilised to evacuate from RUMILLY to IIIrd Corps Main dressing Station

13. Instructions regarding the duties in action of Regimental Medical Officers, Officers Commanding Cavalry Field Ambulances and of the Pack Mounted Sections have already been indicated

14. Advanced Dressing Station & Regimental Aid Posts in the Infantry Area as under

Reference Map 1/40,000 Sheet 5½c

20th Division

Regimental Aid Posts	R.20.a.2.9. (XVI Ravine)
	R.25.d.4.9.
Relay Posts	R.25.a.8.4. (Hotel Cecil)
	R.19.d.3. (near XV RAVINE)
Advanced dressing Station	GOUZEAUCOURT Q.36.d.6.9.

14 cont'd. after ZERO hour others will be established at R.20.a.5.9. and at R.26.c.4.9.

Walking Wounded Station. GOUZEAUCOURT. Q.36.B.1.4. at ZERO hour Advanced Regimental Aid posts will be opened at :— R.20.d.4.4. and R.14.a.8.9.

12th Division

Regimental Aid Posts .... R.26.d.4.1. R.33.b.8.5.
R.34.c.3.9.
(Cheshire Quarry)

Advanced Dressing Station. VILLERS-GUISLAINS)
X.9.a.3.4.

6th Division

Regimental Aid Posts. BEAUCAMP } Map Ref
VILLERS-PLOUICH } not available

Advanced Dressing Station — Advanced.
Q.30.b.2.8.
IIIrd. Corps Main dressing Station and collecting Post for walking wounded is at V.18.c.0.4. on FINS. NURLU. Road.

15. ~~Acknowledge~~

Appendix No. 4

The following are Medical arrangements while in this area:

British Sick will be evacuated to No. 41 Stationary Hospital GAILLY

Infectious Cases to No. 56 C.C.S. EDGEHILL

Medical Stores:- No. 34 A Depot ALBERT

Scabies:- DOIGNT

Mobile Laboratories No. 18 at EDGEHILL

X Ray:- No. 8 Mobile Unit at ACHIE, LE GRAND

Eye Cases:- To No. 3 CCS at GREVILLERS

Indians:- To Lucknow CCS at PERONNE

104 Malose Field Amb, F.A.

Dec. 1917.

Army Form C. 2118.

(199)

WAR DIARY
or
INTELLIGENCE SUMMARY.
(Erase heading not required.)

Army Form C. 2118.

"Revised"

Instructions regarding War Diaries and Intelligence Summaries are contained in F.S. Regs., Part II. and the Staff Manual respectively. Title pages will be prepared in manuscript.

Vol XXXVIII

December 1917

Place	Date	Hour	Summary of Events and Information	Remarks and references to Appendices
Sh 57c 1/40,000 VILLERS FAUCON	1917 Dec 1st		Post section reported tent section disbanded. 24 bearers made up 27/11/41 to VILLERS FAUCON & wheeled carrier placed up at 5 a.m. During the day there were picked up incoming Villers Fau to Lihtdraw to REVELON FARM. Out posts [worked?] by 27/11/41 at W.6.d. All arrangements for evacuation of wounded completed before 3rd hours 3 such as ambulances & three hand ambulances concentrated at HEUDICOURT under Capt = [?]T & WORLEY. Wounded carried by hand to REVELON FARM thence by wheeled carriers to HEUDICOURT. At 11 am [horsed?] ambulance [relieved?] wheeled carriers at the [?] Motor ambulances relieved these the way in beared was 2½ Kilometers. Stretcher each squad did journey inward about 40 Kilometres for the day under [shell fire?] frequently ordinance wounded 80 stretcher cases evacuated + up to 5:30 am. deft & 350 wounded in all were evacuated by the ADS.	P.' officers Commanding 104 (Wilton Indian C) [?] AMBALA B.F. Lt. unreadable being [?] [?] Tank [Corps]. German Prisoners & 1st Division. In addition many [?] walking wounded directed straight to HEUDICOURT Brigade was relieved at 5 am. by 3rd/BAD B.E. and proportional of [?] AD personnel then withdrew to HEUDICOURT
Each Over[?]				

WAR DIARY or INTELLIGENCE SUMMARY

Army Form C. 2118.

Vol XXXVII

Place	Date	Hour	Summary of Events and Information	Remarks and references to Appendices
VILLERS FAUCON	Dec 3rd		A.D.S. marched to VILLERS FAUCON at 9.30am where orders were received from Divn to stand to till escort arrived from Divn	
do	Dec 4th	Mid day	Glen day	
		10.15 a.m.	Orders received for brigade to move to support line (Scheme) + at 2pm also the 2nd line front line escort GAUCHE WOOD to leave 3 motor lorries 3 horsed ambulances with Capt HASSARD with Capt WOLFE – DRS at HEUDECOURT at 5pm DRBHAM with four squads proceeded to REVELON FARM at 6pm some found to cart and posts in addition remaining behind at A+S of 2nd Cav Div in HEUDECOURT	
		Even Dec 5th	The [Scramble?] was not received during the night MAJOR MATTHEWS returned from leave. At 7am 2nd Bn who had gone to relieve East Alden Ditch with 14th 48TH.Bn [returned?], he executed to [Bapeal?]. A.D.S. reported headquarters at midnight with the brigade which was relieved by 9th + 21st Dragoons One wretch was received	
do	Dec 6th	Evn	Five transport arrived On [ribly?] were evacuated Lee day	

Army Form C. 2118.

WAR DIARY
or
INTELLIGENCE SUMMARY.
(Erase heading not required.)

Army Form C. 2118.

Instructions regarding War Diaries and Intelligence Vol XXXVIII
Summaries are contained in F. S. Regs., Part II.
and the Staff Manual respectively. Title pages
will be prepared in manuscript.

1074 M 1470 W 1 8 7 4.

Place	Date	Hour	Summary of Events and Information	Remarks and references to Appendices
VILLERS FAUCON	Dec 7th		Horse transport exercise	
	Even		Capt WORLEY on 3 weeks special leave to England	
	Dec 8th		Quiet cold day	
BRUSLE			Ambulance reached at 12.45 p.m. received at BRUSLE at 3.45 p.m.	
	Even		Wet day	
do	Dec 9th		Horse transport exercise. Capt I & M FIRTH left for duty with 5th Cav Reserve Regt.	
			Sick of brigade collected prior to admission to SEC BAD/1.C.3 A	
	Even		Wet day	
do	Dec 10th		Orders received for advanced dressing station to stand to from 6.30 to 8 a.m.	
			Pay received issued	
	Clear		Fine cold day	
do	Dec 11th		Order for stand to as for yesterday.	
			Bullock cha[rge]	
do	Dec 12th		Order for stand to as for dec 10th	
			Lce[?] KISHEN SINGH on temporary duty with dismounted unmounted[?] at BRUSLE	
	Even		Milder	

2353 Wt. W2544/1454 700,000 5/15 D.D.&L. A.D.S.S./Forms/C. 2118.

Army Form C. 2118.

WAR DIARY
or
INTELLIGENCE SUMMARY.

(Erase heading not required.)

Vol XXVII p 4
105TH M.H.W. / C For

Place	Date	Hour	Summary of Events and Information	Remarks and references to Appendices
BRUGE	Dec 13th		Orders received at 3 am that brigade will be saddled up & ready to move at once after 7 am. At 10 am orders received to off saddle. No ready to move at one hours notice. Orders from advanced divisional section to move in rear of brigade if advanced off & ready over at K3 central water.	
do	Dec 14th	Dawn	Horse transport services open for rest of Brigade till relieved 3rd Dec 14.	
		Dawn	Temporary duty with 1st F.E & Brigd (?) Ottr. best training NC.	
do	Dec 15th		Bull day	
			Horse transport services. On horse being removed had remaining NC 8 Servic A.B.C promoted to Lieut. Action distinguished - been troops in an inmiserable duties for gallantry in the attack.	
do	Dec 16th	Dawn	Church parade. Such morning. B of R. 2. IO Pz. On officer detached.	
		Dawn	Heavy snowstorm.	
do	Dec 17th		Horse transport services. Hat reviewed R.P.D. 17.6.	
		Dawn	Very cold fine day.	

Army Form C. 2118.

WAR DIARY
or
INTELLIGENCE SUMMARY

Vol XXXVII P 5 — 2.2
104 MHOW IDiv

(Erase heading not required.)

Instructions regarding War Diaries and Intelligence Summaries are contained in F. S. Regs., Part II. and the Staff Manual respectively. Title Pages will be prepared in manuscript.

Place	Date	Hour	Summary of Events and Information	Remarks and references to Appendices
BRUAY	Dec 18"		Horse transport exercised. One GSWGT evacuated sick. Still recovering BORS IORG	
do	Dec 19"	Drew Drew	Very cold frosty day. Horse transport exercised. Isolated frost in posterior bosh recurring B 376 IORG. Very cold frosty day	
do	Dec 20"		Horse transport exercised. Frost recurring BORS IORG.	
do	Dec 21"	Drew	Very cold frosty day. Horse transport exercised. Half recurring BOR5 IOR4. Very cold foggy day	
do	Dec 22nd	Drew	Ambulance marched to TERTRY (from STOUENTRY) distance transferred 6 SEUBOR 1 OR2. Arrived TERTRY 11.30 am. and tents erected.	
TERTRY	Dec 23rd	Drew	Horse transport exercised. Fine day.	
do	Dec 24"	Drew	Horse transport exercised. One being hand disinfected. Fine day.	
do	Dec 25"		Wet Cold day.	

Army Form C. 2118.

WAR DIARY
or
INTELLIGENCE SUMMARY

Vol XXVIII O.C. O.C. 10TH M.HOW. 1.0.T.C.

(Erase heading not required.)

Place	Date	Hour	Summary of Events and Information	Remarks and references to Appendices
TERTRY	Dec 26th		Horse transport received. Capt HAZARD M.C. Recd on temporary duty with SECOND I.O.T.C + Capt COLLINS Recd repaired. Cold day.	
do	Dec 27th		Horse transport exercise. One A.E.M.T. evacuated sick medical front inspection Fine day.	
do	Dec 28th		Horse transport exercise. One unit evacuated Cold day.	
do	Dec 29th		Horse transport exercise. Pay received received. Cold very fine cold day.	
do	Dec 30th		One ldr O.R. evacuated sick Fine day.	
do	Dec 31st		Horse transport exercise Fine cold day.	

D. A. Whittaker
Major M.S.
Comdg 10TH M.HOW. 1.0.T.C.

104th Field Ambulance, F.A.

Jan. 1918

Medical

Army Form C. 2118.

WAR DIARY
or
INTELLIGENCE SUMMARY

XXXIX

(Erase heading not required.)

Instructions regarding War Diaries and Intelligence Summaries are contained in F.S. Regs., Part II. and the Staff Manual respectively. Title Pages will be prepared in manuscript.

Place	Date	Hour	Summary of Events and Information	Remarks and references to Appendices
TERTRY	Jan 1st		Horse transport exercise. Tent sections open for AV.MS & W.S. Public bath. One tailor's shop. One laundry received from 5th Cav Sanitary Section. Two A.S.C H.T joined from base. Still remaining Nil. Cold dry day.	A.9.O.I. Steps for support for front line.
do	Jan 2nd		Horse transport exercise. Medical inspection. One A.S.C.M.T admitted received. Still remaining B.O.R 4. I.O.R Nil. Fine cold day.	App II from the medical arrangement
do	Jan 3rd		Horse transport exercise. One Rank rome ward nicely to derby belongs for duty. Still remaining B.O.R. 9 I.O.R. Nil. Pay received received.	
do	Jan 4th		Horse transport exercise. Capt WORLEY Rance. returned from leave to U.K. One went nicely to LUCKNOW C.F.A. for duty. Sick remaining B.O.R 10. I.O.R 1. Fine cold day.	
do	Jan 5th		Horse transport exercise. One Rank permit to from nor to 13th M.G.S. for duty. Ruled sick transferred to See BAD.L.O.J.A. Open for Ireland only. One A.S.C H.T. returned from hospital. Sick remaining B.O.R. Nil I.O.R 6. Fine cold day.	
Dalme				

2449 Wt. W14957/M90 750,000 1/16 J.B.C. & A. Forms/C.2118/12.

Army Form C. 2118.

WAR DIARY
or
INTELLIGENCE SUMMARY

(Erase heading not required.)

Vol XXXIX P 2 O.C.
15th M/HOW. I.O.T.A.

Instructions regarding War Diaries and Intelligence Summaries are contained in F.S. Regs., Part II. and the Staff Manual respectively. Title Pages will be prepared in manuscript.

Place	Date	Hour	Summary of Events and Information	Remarks and references to Appendices
TERTRY	Jan 6th		Capt COLLINS R.A.M.C. now works Ambulance to Dist School Suffrement 1 OR 9. One wound slightly reported from LUCKNOW O.3.a. Kit Inspection.	
do	Jan 7th	Dully	Fine cold day—	
			Horse transport exercise. Been regroundes inspection. One horse cast ground for duty from R.C.H.A. Sick remaining 1 OR 9. ADS a one hour notice to move out.	
do	Jan 8th	Colder	Wet mild day—	
			Horse transport exercise. Sick remaining 1 OR 9.	
do	Jan 9th		Frost.....	
			Horse transport exercise. 1 ACO. M.T. reported from hospital PTE 15. Sick remaining 1 OR 11.	
		Colder	Frost.....	
do	Jan 10th		Horse transport exercise. Sgt Major SPROLE R.H.M.G. evacuated sick. Sick remaining 1 OR 11. Pay received.	
		Dulley	Cold dry day—	
do	Jan 11th		Horse transport exercise. Sick remaining 1 OR 15.	
		Dulley	Cold damp day—	

Army Form C. 2118.

WAR DIARY

INTELLIGENCE SUMMARY

Vol XXXIX p 3

(Erase heading not required.)

Instructions regarding War Diaries and Intelligence Summaries are contained in F.S. Regs., Part II. and the Staff Manual respectively. Title Pages will be prepared in manuscript.

Place	Date	Hour	Summary of Events and Information	Remarks and references to Appendices
TERTRY	Jan 12th	Day	Horse transport received. Sick remaining 12 I.O.R.	
			Orders received that Indian units will proceed East.	
			Cold wet day.	
do	Jan 13th	Day	Inspection by D.D.M.S. Cav. Corps. Sick remaining 1 O.R. 12	
			Cold wet day.	
do	Jan 14th		Horse transport received. Two mules evacuated. Bone regnts. purchased	
			inspection. Sick remaining 1 O.R. 17.	
			Cold wet day.	
do	Jan 15th	Day	Horse transport received. Two mules evacuated. Sick remaining 1 O.R. 13.	
			Heavy gale rain.	
do	Jan 16th	Day	Horse transport received. Sick remaining 1 O.R. 10.	
			Gale rain.	
do	Jan 17th	Day	Horse transport received. Sick remaining 1 O.R. 15. Pay received received	
			2/Lt S. Booth N.Mundan Corr. Horse Keeper to Woolwich R.A. for temporary duty	
			Mild wet day.	
do	Jan 18th	Day	Horse transport received. Sick remaining 1 O.R. 11	
			Damp mild day	

Army Form C. 2118.

WAR DIARY
or
INTELLIGENCE SUMMARY p 4 one

(Erase heading not required.)

Vol XXXIX   107/M/HW/1CTd

Instructions regarding War Diaries and Intelligence Summaries are contained in F. S. Regs, Part II. and the Staff Manual respectively. Title Pages will be prepared in manuscript.

Place	Date	Hour	Summary of Events and Information	Remarks and references to Appendices
TERTNY	Jan 19th		Horse transport exercise. One A.S.C. M.T. proceeded from HQ 5th Cav Supply Column. Still remaining 1 off. 11.	
do	Jan 20th		Quiet day.	
do	Jan 21		Kit inspection. Still remaining 1 off. 9.	
do	Jan 22nd		Held day.	
do	Jan V.M.		Horse transport exercise. Still remaining 1 off. 12	
do			Held day. None ran.	
do	Jan 23rd		Horse transport exercise. Medical inspection 1 cook reported from LUCKNOW R.O. Still remaining 1 off. 10.	
do	Sat 23rd		Held day.	
do	Jan 23rd		Horse transport exercise. Orders received to proceed into the line about 26 Jany. Still remaining 1 off. P. 40.	
do	Sun 24		Held day.	
do	Jan 24		Horse transport exercise. Am replenishing with one horse. Dvr KISSHEN SINGH reported the sweeper chose to return to India. Still remaining 1 off. 10.	
do			Pay received — nominal.	
do	Jan 25th		Held day.	
do			Horse transport exercise. Still remaining 1 off. 7	
do			Held day — none ran.	

Army Form C. 2118.

WAR DIARY or INTELLIGENCE SUMMARY

(Erase heading not required.)

Vol XXXIX   P5 OC
                             104 M/How 10 7 R

Place	Date	Hour	Summary of Events and Information	Remarks and references to Appendices
BIHECOURT STATION R20d94	Jan 26	4	H.Q. of ambulance moved to BIHECOURT STATION after closing intervening RAP to Sec Bad (C.7.a. around 5 pm) tacking over from 3rd C.F.A. one A.D.S. under Capt HASSARD M.C. @ JEANCOURT (L26d11) & one A.D.S. (L26d11) & one A.D.S. under Capt WORSLEY @ VADENCOURT (R16a93) relieving similar units of 2nd C.F.A. 6 A.B.C. to R.A.P at R11a2& for right sub sector. 4 A.B.C at L33 F50 RAP for left sub-sector - Capt COLLINS rejoined from 5th Can Div School	App III Personnel rearrangement App IV Personnel of MDS.
		Clear cool foggy day		
do	Jan 27	Clear	Nil - One C.A.M.C officer & 2 CAMC OR joined for temporary duty from Canadian Cas Pol Sub	
		foggy day		
do	Jan 28	Clear	Nil	
		foggy day		
do	Jan 29	Clear Dull day	Nil Two A.B.O one messenger joined from leave	
do	Jan 30	Dull Rainy day	Nil Clear fine day	
do	Jan 31	Cold foggy day	Nil one A.B.O evacuated sick	

D Quinn Lieut.
Major Q.M.
At (and)? 104 M/How, C.F.A.

Appendix No I

Table of Duties of Brigades

1.	2.	3.	4.	5.	6.
Brigade	27th December to 12 noon Jan 1st	12 noon Jan 1st to 12 noon Jan 7th	12 noon Jan 7th to 12 noon Jan 13th	12 noon Jan 13th to 12 noon Jan 19th	12 noon Jan 19th to 12 noon Jan 25th
Ambala Cavalry Brigade	Working Party for 24th Division	Required to occupy the line R.O.M. R.2.w.0.y.	One hour's notice to act as mounted reserve to Debionaire Division	As in Column 2	As in Column 3
1. (a)	x	x	x	x	x
(b)	x	x	x	x	x

(c) Indian Field Ambulance (less Tent Section) will concentrate at TERTRY Cross Roads ESTREE - VERMAND - CAULAINCOURT - POEUILLY and having its arrival to Brigade Report Centre at Cemetery Q.29.c.y.4. it will proceed to SOYECOURT Cross Roads Q.24.b.8.4. On receipt of further orders and before its arrival there to Brigade Report Centre, MONTOLU WOODS No. 2. R.14.b.o.b.

In the case of A.T. Troops the Brigade (less Tent Section in Non F.A.) will parade as follows:—

2.

(a) In Non Field Ambulance In Billets below y Road

"Appendix II"

Extract from Cavalry Corps Medical
Arrangements Operations No. 19 dated 14th Dec. 1917

Map Reference 62C /Roya

2. The location of Medical Units in the front line
forward Area are shewn hereunder
Left Sub-Sector   Centre Sub-Sector

(I) Regimental Aid Posts
F.23.d.35   L.11.b.29   L.23.d.5.3
L.5.c.y.6   L.11.b.34   L.28.a central
L.10.a.central   L.10.c.8.y   R.5.a.8.5

Advanced Dressing Stations

(II) TEMPLEUX-LE-
GUERARD. L.2.c central   JEANCOURT L.26.d.11. VADENCOURT
ROISEL.K.16.d.8.1   R.16.a.9.3.

(iii) Main Dressing Station and Post treatment Centre
    BERNES. Q.4.a.0.5.

(IV) Ambulance Rest Station   DOINGT

(V) Corps Scabies Station
    72 Field Ambulance
    Corps Rest Station   BERNES

(VI) 1st Cavalry Field Ambulance. CAPPY

Appendix III

Extract from 5" Cav: Div: Operation Order Medical No: 14

Equipment from MHOW I CFA

12 Field Stretchers
50 Ammonia Capsules
1 Gallon Whale Oil
5 lbs Oxford Grease
5 lbs Oxford Powder

Transport and Equipment as for AMBALA Dismounted Brigade the 12 Field Stretchers to be found by MHOW I CFA. The Lance pattern Regimental Stretcher will not be taken into the line.

(2) O.C. MHOW I CFA will take over the Advanced Dressing Station of both Sub-sectors at JEANCOURT and VADENCOURT respectively, with his Head Quarters at BIHECOURT, relieving No: 3 C.F.A. Advance parties to report at JEANCOURT and VADENCOURT by noon 26" inst: Relief to be completed by midnight January 26"/27". Two Motor Ambulances and one cyclist will be posted at each A.D.S; remainder of Ambulance transport will be at BIHECOURT and available as occasion demands.

(3) O.C. Canadian CFA will place 1 Medical Officer, and 2 other ranks at the disposal of O.C. MHOW I CFA, as a temporary measure. They will report at TERTRY noon January 26th.

(4) The Regimental Aid Posts for Right Sub-Sector is in Cooker's Quarry R.11.a.8.4. Forward Aid Post at R.6.a. central, R.4.d.7.9, and M.7.6.0.6. are available when necessary. The Regimental Aid Posts for Left Sub-Sector are the Quarry at L.28.c.5.8., R.5.a.7.5. and at L.33.d.3.9. which last will be considered as a Relay Post for the Regimental Aid Post at R.5.a.7.5.

(5) The transport of all wounded unable to walk is by hand under Regimental Arrangements from the line to R.A.P., thence by Bearer parties with wheeled carriers to the A.D.S.

(6) All wounded will be sent to the Corps M.D.S. BERNES except urgent cases requiring immediate surgical attention e.g. wounds of head & abdomen which will be evacuated to TINCOURT in the case of British Ranks and to TINCOURT in the case of Indians direct.

(7) British Sick will be sent to No. 4. C.F.A. at POEUILLY, Indian Sick to ST. CREN.

List of Personnel
Appendix IV

A.D.S L.26 d.1.1		A.D.S R.16 a.9.3	
Officers	2	Officers	3
S.A.S	1	S.S.A.S	1
S.W.O	1	S.W.O	1
W.S.	1	W.S.	1
Cook	1	Cook	1
Sweeper	1	Sweeper	1
A.B.C	22	A.B.C	20
Private RAMC	1	Nursing Orderly	1
" CAMC	1	Private CAMC	1
ASC MT	4	ASC MT	3
ASC HT	2		

Office copy

Feb. 1918.

CONFIDENTIAL.

WAR DIARY

OF

(UNIT) Offr. i/c (Albany Sec.) Field Ambulance E.E. Force.

(PERIOD) 1st February 1918 TO 28th February 1918.

VOLUME XL

No. 1 Coy. A.
1 Coy.
Base

Army Form C. 2118.

WAR DIARY
or
INTELLIGENCE SUMMARY

(Erase heading not required.)

Officer Commanding
104 M/I O W Indian Cavalry Field Ambulance

VOLUME XL

Instructions regarding War Diaries and Intelligence Summaries are contained in F. S. Regs., Part II. and the Staff Manual respectively. Title Pages will be prepared in manuscript.

Stamp: BASE EMBARK. (INDIAN SECTION) 30 MAY 1918 G.H.Q.E.

Place	Date	Hour	Summary of Events and Information	Remarks and references to Appendices
Marseille	1918			
EMBARK STATION	Feb 1st		Horse transport arrived	
MARSEILLES	Feb 2nd		Cold day	
do	Feb 3rd		Horse transport arrived. Two A.S.C. M.T. lepers men in France	
do			Clear day	
do	Feb 3rd		Horse transport arrived. One A.S.C. leaves reported from hospital	
do			Clear day	
do	Feb 4th		Horse transport arrived. Pay issued received	
do	Feb 5th		Severe cold day	
do			Horse transport arrived. One A.S.C. leave available U.K.	
do			Clear mild day	
do	Feb 6th		Horse transport arrived	
do			Indian Clear day	
do	Feb 7th		Horse transport arrived. Sub Cond SHEPPERD on leave to U.K.	
do			Clear wet day	
do	Feb 8th		Horse transport arrived. One Syce A.S.M. transferred to No 1 base M.T depot Rouen	
			Very wet day	

Army Form C. 2118.

WAR DIARY
or
INTELLIGENCE SUMMARY

(Erase heading not required.)

Instructions regarding War Diaries and Intelligence Summaries are contained in F. S. Regs, Part II. and the Staff Manual respectively. Title Pages will be prepared in manuscript.

No. 6   O.C. 10th BN 10th

Place	Date	Hour	Summary of Events and Information	Remarks and references to Appendices
BIHUCOURT STATION				

Army Form C. 2118.

WAR DIARY
or
INTELLIGENCE SUMMARY.
(Erase heading not required.)

Vol XL p 3 pA 1cb M1BW ( ) A

Instructions regarding War Diaries and Intelligence Summaries are contained in F. S. Regs., Part II. and the Staff Manual respectively. Title pages will be prepared in manuscript.

Place	Date	Hour	Summary of Events and Information	Remarks and references to Appendices

Army Form C. 2118.

WAR DIARY
or
INTELLIGENCE SUMMARY.
(Erase heading not required.)

104 M.H.W. (C.T.A.)

Instructions regarding War Diaries and Intelligence Summaries are contained in F. S. Regs., Part II. and the Staff Manual respectively. Title pages will be prepared in manuscript.

Vol XL

Place	Date	Hour	Summary of Events and Information	Remarks and references to Appendices
[illegible]	3 [Feb]		Sers & B.1.1. U.R. proceeded by rail to TARANTO.	
	Feb 4		Sunday.	
			Col SUTTON'S return from leave	
	Feb 5		Monday	
			When have received from 8th Lancers 2 miles from ANGONA Signal	
			Lodge third war.	
	Feb 6		Ambulance carried Lt C RUMIGNY serving up from	
	Salerno		Sun day	
			Lt Col SAB MATTHEWS Capt HASSARD returned from leave	
MI G NN) Feb 7 I.R.	Salerno		Last day	
MI CH) 7.0 am			Recd M.S BITHS Lieu I.O.R returned from LUCENA W.C.S	
do Feb LS I.A			Capt HASSARD MC RAMC posted to SEE BAD 16 F.A. + see below. Cavalier 57 A	
			Today Sun day.	

[signatures]
Lt Col [illegible]
Comdg 104 M.H.W. (C.T.A.)

SECRET.   Copy No. 8

VAULT Operation Order No. 1.   Feb 11th 1918.

Medical arrangements for VIPER Operation Order
No. 33 are as follows:-

1. 8 Stretcher bearers from VASE two
Stretcher bearers from VICAR at FISHERS
Crater.

2. SMS ATA MOHOMED with six wheeled
stretchers & 12 bearers provided by VAULT
at Barrier Post.

3. Capt MAGNER, RAMC with one SAS one
ward orderly & 4 bearers 6 spare
stretchers 2 horsed ambulances and
one Ford Car at TWIN Craters
evacuating to ADS. VADENCOURT.

4. Stretchers will be sent out with
two blankets each.

5. No dressing, except of the most urgent
nature will be done at BARRIER Post
all cases being sent on immediately
and the party withdrawn from there
as soon as all wounded have passed
through.

6. ACKNOWLEDGE (Capt MAGNER, RAMC) to
ADS, VADENCOURT only.

Copy No. 1. ADMS BOS
  do   No. 2 TAX.
  do   No. 3 VIPER.   Lieutenant
  do   No. 4 Capt MAGNER. RAMC.   Major
  do   No. 5 OC ADS VADENCOURT.   OC VAULT.
  do   No. 6 & 8 WAR DIARY
  do   No. 9 Office.

Appendix II

With reference to Div. Order S.S. [?] dated February 14 1918 following are medical arrangements:-

(1) An aid post will be established at GRAHAMS POST to which all casualties requiring transport will be carried by hand, and on which all walking wounded should be directed.

Personnel & Equipment as under:-
Capt E.C. WHITEHOUSE MC CRMC
Capt T.C. McCULLOUGH CRMC - This officer is also available if required to supervise evacuation.
1 NCO 3 BOR. and 16 OR. RMOW. 10 FA

Equipment
    Medical Haversack and companions
    4 Haversacks, shell dressings
    50 Spare First Field Dressings
    25 Ammonia Capsules
    8 Wheel'd Stretcher Carriers, complete with Field Stretchers
    Splints assorted, leg and arm.
    2 Thomas' Splints to be included
    8 Spare Field Stretchers
    2 Blankets per stretcher.

(2) A relay and collecting post will be formed at O 20 b.7.8. Personnel which will accompany covering party to O 20 b 7 8 will consist of 1 NCO and 16 stretcher bearers under L/C Mason.

Each man will carry a haversack of shell dressings and one Field Stretcher. The stretchers to be carried at the trail, two by each pair of stretcher bearers, the object being to provide an extra pair of stretchers at the Relay Post. Casualties other than walking wounded will not be carried further than this point by Regt Stretcher Bearers until all wounded have been removed from the enemy's trenches. It is understood that 4 Spare Field Stretchers will be conveyed to this post under Brigade arrangements making 8 Field Stretchers all available here. After any additional First Aid that may be necessary has been rendered at this post, wounded will, as bearers become available and released from duty further forward, be removed to the Aid post at GRAHAMS POST. Prisoners will be made use of freely as circumstances permit.

3) With the landing party there will be 20 stretcher bearers
found as under:-
    12 Regt Stretcher Bearers with normal wheel stretchers
    8 Stretchers on Company Stretcher Bearers who will [illegible]
    4 Stretchers with Rifle and Cork to [illegible]
There will be 2 Stretcher Bearers and 1 wh. Stretcher with each
Flank Guard.

(4) From Stations Post evacuation of wounded requiring [illegible]
will be by Wheeled Carriers to A.D.S. A.D.2., where 3 Carriers
will be posted. Each Station [illegible] [illegible] carry up spare hand
Stretchers as a reserve.

5) Horse Ambulances will ply between A.D.S. A.D.2. and [illegible]
carrying wounded will be posted.

6) [illegible] horse Ambulances will be posted at the A.D.S. [illegible]
one of which will stand by to proceed to base A.D.y, immediately
on the arrival of a loaded ambulance at the A.D.S. without further
[illegible]

7) Arrangement are being made to have 2 motor Ambulances
additional to above posted at [illegible]

Appendix III

With reference to operations to take place tonight please note following instructions and arrangements.

(1) As now directed by DMS 5th Army wounded are to be evacuated to a C.C.S. direct without being passed through a Main Dressing Station.
In consequence all British wounded will be evacuated to TINCOURT and all Indian wounded other than urgent abdominal, chest and head injuries, in normal or improvised Indian trains cannot be taken direct to TINCOURT.

(2) A strong parcel Label fully made out is to be attached to all wounded. All other Base particulars of wounded British & Indian will be furnished on a normal Roll to A.D.S. BEARERS directly on the conclusion of operations.

(2) Owing to these arrangements it will be necessary to ensure that a sufficient supply of splints especially of thigh and leg are provided at both your A.D.Ss.

(3) To assist in evacuation the following motor ambulances, additional to your own, will be available:-

2 Motor Ambulances will report to O.C. MDS TINCOURT at 4 P.M. These should it is suggested be sent back to a fixed position at MONTIGNY FARM. The driver of each loaded car as he passes that place en route to TINCOURT will direct the driver of one of these reserve cars to proceed to JEANCOURT to take his place. The Decauville Railway is also available at JEANCOURT as a means of evacuating wounded. An engine and trucks will be in readiness and the journey to TINCOURT takes two minutes.

(4) For the Right Sub-Sector 6 cars will be posted at the Cavalry Ambulance POEUILLY. The driver of each of your loaded cars as he passes the cross roads, POEUILLY, will notify his arrival before going on when one of these reserve cars will forthwith proceed to MDS VADENCOURT.

(5) If necessary Cavalry Ambulance, POEUILLY will be prepared to reinforce either VADENCOURT or JEANCOURT by 16 Bearers under an NCO. Should occasion demand your moving forward a small Bearer party from either A.D.S.

(b) You should ensure that there is a sufficient reserve of stretchers at each of your HQrs and in horse and motor ambulances belonging to your CoA.

7. 2 Motor Ambulances from Cavalry Ambulance, Rouilly with a reserve of 20 stretchers in each will report to you at Bécourt at 3 p.m.

8. There is telephone communication between you and A.G.S. Divisional Divisions and the following places:-

 (a) C.R.E.   Tinchurst
 (b) Canadian Dismounted Brigade.
 (c) Ambala Dismounted Brigade
 (d) A.D.M.S. Dismounted Division.

9. Refer to these Divisions that any point of difficulty arises and notify conclusion of evacuation of wounded.
        Major General C. Gifling
        ADMS Dismounted Division

CONFIDENTIAL.

WAR DIARY

OF

(UNIT) 104th (MHow) Encl. Aust. Field Artillery. E.E.FORCE.

(PERIOD) 1st March 1918. TO 31st March 1918.

VOLUME XLI

Army Form C.2118

WAR DIARY
or
INTELLIGENCE SUMMARY.

(Erase heading not required.)

Instructions regarding War Diaries and Intelligence Summaries are contained in F.S. Regs., Part II. and the Staff Manual respectively. Title pages will be prepared in manuscript.

Volume XLI

Officer Commanding
104th MHOW Indian Cavalry Field Ambulance

Place	Date	Hour	Summary of Events and Information	Remarks and references to Appendices
ROMIGNY	March 1 1918		Nos. E.A.E. MATTHEWS left for MARSEILLES. Placed under orders of ADMS MARSEILLES for remainder of march entrain at SALEUX for MARSEILLES in march. Men returned for remainder of march, entrained by troop train to TARANTO.	
			Capt HASSAN D. PILOT M.O. proceeded by troop train to TARANTO.	
SALEUX	March 2nd		Snowy day. Remainder of unit entrained SALEUX by 5.30 pm. Capt WORLEY RAMC. temporarily SEC'D AD I.C. F.A.	
	March 3rd		Snowy day.	
	March 4th		En route by troop train to MARSEILLES.	
MARSEILLES	March 5		Arrived 2.30 am. Equipment loaded on lorries and removed, animals marched to MONT FURON Camp. Empty vehicles and stock taken over by advance party.	
			Fine day	
do	March 6		N.d.	
do	March 7	Very heavy	Equipment sent to docks for loading in charge of Cpl ROMANO	
do	March 8	Calm 10.. 11.. 12..	N.J.	
do		Calm Entry	Per Marcel Manuel	
do		13-14 am	N.J.	

Army Form C. 2118.

WAR DIARY
or
INTELLIGENCE SUMMARY.

(Erase heading not required.)

Instructions regarding War Diaries and Intelligence Summaries are contained in F.S. Regs., Part II. and the Staff Manual respectively. Title pages will be prepared in manuscript.

Volume XII No. 2
10th MH on I.C.J.74

Place	Date	Hour	Summary of Events and Information	Remarks and references to Appendices
MARSEILLES	March 15th		Unit moved to LA VALENTINE Camp.	
do	"	Dawn	One mule & two horses unearthed. Fine windy day.	
do	"	16th	B. D'H and A & C. returned from base stud guard. Wet day.	
do	"	17th	Pay received received. Fine day.	
do	"	18th	29 B.O.R. 1 Br NCO 2 1 O.R. + 27 mules embarked. Fine day.	
do	"	19th	2 R. horses 1 mule received from remount depot	
do	"	20th Friday Saturday	Nil	
do	"	21st	Unit moved to No 10 Rest Camp. Pay received received.	
do	"	25 Sunday 29th	Nil	
do	"	30th	One mule destroyed for veterinary reason. Unit embarked on H.M.T. MENOMINEE.	
do	"	31st	Nil	

[signature]
Lt Col hy
Cmdg 10th MH on I.C.J.A

BEF

4 Cav Div

Troops

Sialcot Cav Fld Amb

1917 Jan - 1918 Apr

To Egypt 4 Cav Div Troops

SERIAL No. 240

Confidential

War Diary

of

SIALKOT CAVALRY FIELD AMBULANCE — 4th Cavalry Division

COMMITTEE FOR THE
MEDICAL HISTORY OF THE WAR
Date 23 APR. 1917

FROM 1st JANUARY 1917. TO 31st JANUARY 1917.

Army Form C. 2118.

Original

● WAR DIARY
or
● INTELLIGENCE SUMMARY Vol XXIV
(Erase heading not required.)

Instructions regarding War Diaries and Intelligence Summaries are contained in F. S. Regs., Part II. and the Staff Manual respectively. Title Pages will be prepared in manuscript.

Place	Date	Hour	Summary of Events and Information	Remarks and references to Appendices
MEAULTE	1.1.17		Pte Bone reported from sick at 9 BMS Rgue. Received from XIV Corps No 656/9/15 re Prophylaxis and Preventive of Trench feet, which the entomology considered the statement adopted by the French approx. the experience of BMS 9 & 658 the re prophylactic use of anti tetanus serum in war injuries is full of the statistics.	
"	2.1.17		Understood that all the hospital sent to respect from their ambulances not to send to the field ambulances but that received beyond there when requested orders to billets tonight.	
"	3.1.17		Received from Field Cashier £125.0.5.7. Paid allowance to men. Forty minor operations on G.O.s receiving instructions to the men required in my med. Received No 3566 BMS company Inspector change in Institution.	
"	4.1.17		Pte Munro invalided via steam to UK. On leave. to 7 and observer outfit received today from men and returned in the afternoon	

Army Form C. 2118.

WAR DIARY
or
INTELLIGENCE SUMMARY

(Erase heading not required.)

Instructions regarding War Diaries and Intelligence Summaries are contained in F. S. Regs, Part II. and the Staff Manual respectively. Title Pages will be prepared in manuscript.

Place	Date	Hour	Summary of Events and Information	Remarks and references to Appendices
MEAULTE	4.1.17		B.R.O. N° 2031 re Discipline on Leave and 2042-44 re "Censorship brought to notice of all O.C.'s	
	5.1.17		Received Orders re Treatment of slight inflammatory affections	
	6.1.17		Information received that O.N.C. No [illegible] to be promoted to the Rank Grade of S.M. Rgt received - O.M.S. No 412 - Instructions re limitation of leave & amount of leave granted to those proceeded on quart leave to India	
	7.1.17		Reported that it was not possible[?] necessary to ensure all Western Field Trench Box to that of 1916 field battalions and batteries followed on line of advance with every detail. [illegible] of Infantry Brigade seven selected back to Camp. Moved Paris ALBERT.	
	8.1.17		Orders regarding Supply Pay[?] of Change in Strength[?] of A.S.M. Si. the changes in infantry Brigade & [illegible] in the certain Westion[?] re supply of [illegible] French bread	

2449 Wt. W14957/Mgo 750,000 1/16 J.B.C. & A. Forms/C.2118/12.

WAR DIARY or INTELLIGENCE SUMMARY

Army Form C. 2118.

(Erase heading not required.)

Instructions regarding War Diaries and Intelligence Summaries are contained in F. S. Regs., Part II. and the Staff Manual respectively. Title Pages will be prepared in manuscript.

Place	Date	Hour	Summary of Events and Information	Remarks and references to Appendices
MEAJITE	9.1.17		Amir Feb's brother to leave for D.K. Mudowia by 17.00hrs. WAHAB has been ordered to the Sahia front.	
	10.1.17		Reserve hostel opened Sughr 1.1.17. 18 men of A.B. Corps sent on with First Battn. Sughr. Proceed Kumbar. Information received that about 70 Colorado LAMB is promised reinforcement from 19.11.15 O.H.	
	11.1.17		Information received that the Turks sent information to the Division area to show importance of the position. Instructions issued to two Battn. at.....? in Map MEAJITE. 19 Indian was ordered this morning. The Corps of KAWAN proceed to MEAJITE. Situation reported that at Field HQ....at one billets accept earlier than limit.	
	12.1.17		Situation normally. Members of every day in army by dusk until.... on enforcing law........ ...reading that he been used of SUBJECT	

Army Form C. 2118.

WAR DIARY
or
INTELLIGENCE SUMMARY
(Erase heading not required.)

Instructions regarding War Diaries and Intelligence Summaries are contained in F.S. Regs., Part II. and the Staff Manual respectively. Title Pages will be prepared in manuscript.

Place	Date	Hour	Summary of Events and Information	Remarks and references to Appendices
HEDAUTE	12.1.17		Anthrome time 10 Sean district from [illegible] [illegible] [illegible] [illegible] [illegible] entirely consumed from [illegible] at 3.30 [illegible] [illegible] [illegible] located ran aid of day. No enemy [illegible] [illegible] rain only further train [illegible] [illegible]	
BOUBERT	13.1.17		Enemy opened at HEDAUTE - WONCOURT at 3 a.m. Retaining commenced at [illegible] turn on enemies at 3.15 a.m. Worked [illegible] out 9.45 a.m. [illegible] [illegible] [illegible] The hostile [illegible] assisted by [illegible] their [illegible] [illegible] the Artillery did not take part in the [illegible] [illegible] Wham Brigade.	
	14.1.17	10.15 a.m	K RAMAN reported his tempest at 5th Can Division O.C. Brigade [illegible] [illegible] [illegible] [illegible] dead [illegible] 2 [illegible] [illegible] M.B [illegible] [illegible] C.F.A. One to help and H.B company [illegible] [illegible] [illegible] [illegible] [illegible] [illegible] C.F.A. Cannon [illegible] [illegible] and [illegible] Shelton and [illegible] Regiment [illegible] [illegible] [illegible]	

Army Form C. 2118.

WAR DIARY
or
INTELLIGENCE SUMMARY
(Erase heading not required.)

Place	Date	Hour	Summary of Events and Information	Remarks and references to Appendices
BOULOGNE	15.1.17		On L.D. Kline erected for Sisters. Rounds of Wards.	
	16.1.17		Consolidated and improved wards to cope with great increase of sick. Ambulances received and despatched daily the wounded & sick being passed on to the Base hospitals, or through the harbour to England. Officers i/c Wards. Major MEADE. Lady Superintendent Miss SHIELD. Night Superintendent Miss HUNGERFORD (?), Doctor P. Raby, S. Day, P. Night. Matron has kept a diary containing more detail of work at Base.	

(illegible notes at bottom)

Army Form C. 2118.

WAR DIARY
or
INTELLIGENCE SUMMARY

(Erase heading not required.)

Instructions regarding War Diaries and Intelligence Summaries are contained in F. S. Regs., Part II. and the Staff Manual respectively. Title Pages will be prepared in manuscript.

Place	Date	Hour	Summary of Events and Information	Remarks and references to Appendices
BOUBERT	16.1.17			
	17.1.17			
	18.1.17			
	19.1.17			
	20.1.17			
	21.1.17			

WAR DIARY
or
INTELLIGENCE SUMMARY

(Erase heading not required.)

Army Form C. 2118.

Place	Date	Hour	Summary of Events and Information	Remarks and references to Appendices
BOULOGNE	22/1/17		[illegible]	
	23/1/17		Battalion have arranged a [illegible]	
	24/1/17		O.C. [illegible]	
	25/1/17		[illegible]	
	26/1/17		[illegible]	
	27/1/17		[illegible]	
	28/1/17		[illegible]	

Army Form C. 2118.

WAR DIARY
or
INTELLIGENCE SUMMARY
(Erase heading not required.)

Instructions regarding War Diaries and Intelligence Summaries are contained in F.S. Regs., Part II. and the Staff Manual respectively. Title Pages will be prepared in manuscript.

Place	Date	Hour	Summary of Events and Information	Remarks and references to Appendices
BOUBERT	29.4.17		Accompanied Brig. Gen'l. to reconnoitre route B to B to follow in an operation proposed in event of enemy retiring. Route found difficult on account of woods & streams across it.	
	30.4.17		Visits to Kala wounds and sick parade. Visited 1st Cav. Inf: H.Q. & A & M.S. No 32. Visits made at followed for men reasons to stay.	
	31.4.17		—	

Com'd: Stalcote Cav: Fd Amb:
1st Ind: Cav: Divs:

Medical

Serial No: 240

4. Cavalry Div.

to 28.2.17

COMMITTEE FOR THE
MEDICAL HISTORY OF THE WAR
Date 21 MAY 1917

Vol XXV

Original

Confidential

War Diary

of

CAVALRY FIELD AMBULANCE
SIALKOTE

Feb/17

from 1.2.17

Army Form C. 2118.

Medical

Original

WAR DIARY
or
INTELLIGENCE SUMMARY

(Erase heading not required.)

Vol XXV

Instructions regarding War Diaries and Intelligence Summaries are contained in F. S. Regs., Part II. and the Staff Manual respectively. Title Pages will be prepared in manuscript.

Place	Date	Hour	Summary of Events and Information	Remarks and references to Appendices
BOMBERT	1.2.17		Ordered that all spare shoes on the above cars on to be filled both noses. Received ADMS No 336 re Toxicological Specimens.	M
"	2.2.17		Sweeper LIMBA transferred to Lucknow CFA under arrangements from ADMS. Received ADMS No 356 re Hiring of Buildings. ADMS visited the Unit.	M
"	3.2.17		Lieut. Kalapurwalla & Zaman returned from Ontigao School. Received ADMS No 357 & 367 re Sao France and Veterinary arrangements in an advance.	M
"	4.2.17		Lieut Kalapurwalla transferred for temporary Relief at Sperry of Xanier. Cir. No 374 re Field Medical Equipment received	M
"	5.2.17		One British and one Indian NCO attended for distance of Corps & Do. Order re Speedy of Motor Ambulances instituted in regimental orders.	M
"	6.2.17		Still very hard frost. Standing Orders for Unit circulated on the Order Book	M

J. Johnson
Major

Army Form C. 2118.

WAR DIARY
or
INTELLIGENCE SUMMARY

(Erase heading not required.)

Instructions regarding War Diaries and Intelligence Summaries are contained in F. S. Regs., Part II. and the Staff Manual respectively. Title Pages will be prepared in manuscript.

Place	Date	Hour	Summary of Events and Information	Remarks and references to Appendices
BOUBERT	7.2.17		A.D.M.S. No 4119 re "GHQ" received and circulated. Also No 4118 "War Establishment" and No 4119 "Training Areas"	JM
"	8.2.17		— — — —	
"	9.2.17		Motor Ambulance car returned from duty with 6th M.S. Cav. Corps.	JM
"	10.2.17		Recd. A.D.M.S. No 446 re 'Captured Guns'	JM
"	11.2.17		A.D.M.S. No 448 of 10.2.17 re Censorship orders read out on parade to all ranks; A.D.M.S. No 452 re Trench Relief by troops took part in hand at war.	JM
"	12.2.17		Driver Hanrahan evacuated to General Hospital. Strength of strength two rations of Indian personnel supplied	JM
"	13.2.17		Certified that order re Censorship has been read out on parade. Recd. No 4756 B.M.S. re New movement sign	JM
"	14.2.17		— — — —	
"	15.2.17		Received A.A.& Circular No 46/49. Wand.Serv. of non-comm. B.C.S. in strength. All the strength. Bath sent B.S.R. of signatures.	JM

2449 Wt. W14957/M90 759,000 1/16 J.B.C. & A. Forms/C.2118/12.

Army Form C. 2118.

WAR DIARY
or
INTELLIGENCE SUMMARY

(Erase heading not required.)

Instructions regarding War Diaries and Intelligence Summaries are contained in F. S. Regs., Part II. and the Staff Manual respectively. Title Pages will be prepared in manuscript.

Place	Date	Hour	Summary of Events and Information	Remarks and references to Appendices
BOUBERT	15.2.17		Received ADMS N° 498 re "Return of arrivals for agricultural work".	
"	16.2.17		Pte Malette evacuated to CCS in which 11 the absence of Cook Sergt Babot required in cooking from CCS	
"	17.2.17		Received ADMS M/s 511 & 512 re Divisional orders for vehicles and Dress of Warrant Officers Class II	
"	18.2.17			
"	19.2.17		Thaw scheme came into operation in Divisional area. Reported to ADMS the number of Officers who have gone through Anti-gas course. Reported that the billeting wards have through- out in the area occupied by the Unit.	
"	20.2.17		Received ADMS N° 558 - Road space of Unit - this will be actually measured	
"	21.2.17		The road space of the Unit by actual measurement amounts to 219 yards - excluding Motor Ambulances and Monthly herds	
"	22.2.17		Received instructions re thaw scheme and Traffic that for new Thaw Scheme	

Army Form C. 2118.

WAR DIARY
or
INTELLIGENCE SUMMARY

(Erase heading not required.)

Instructions regarding War Diaries and Intelligence Summaries are contained in F. S. Regs., Part II. and the Staff Manual respectively. Title Pages will be prepared in manuscript.

Place	Date	Hour	Summary of Events and Information	Remarks and references to Appendices
BOUBERT	23.2.17		Received A.D.M.S. N° 590 & "Shortage of Khaki" and 593 re conference of Echelons. Reported that all Smoke Helmets have been inspected & found defective nature.	
"	24.2.17		Driver WILSON A.S.C. H.T. joined for duty with the Unit	
"	25.2.17		Received N° 612 A.D.M.S. S.R.O. N° 2142 - Captured German Sig Book communicated to all ranks	
WARGNIES	26.2.17		Orders received at 1.15 a.m. that the Ambulance would be required to move at short notice. Orders issued to have all carts ready by daylight. Horses to be watered 5 a.m. bringing the S.S. Wagon and Horse Ambulance from the Divisional Workshop. Orders received at 6.20 a.m. that the Ambulance in proceeding towards the front line with Lucknow Brigade and to be at MOYENNEVILLE at 10.30 a.m. The Unit left BOUBERT for say with exception 1 m S.S. Wagon, no Horse Ambulance and Water Transport. Arrived at MOYENNEVILLE at 10.35 a.m. Left at 12.5X and arrived on billets at WARGNIES at 8.15 p.m. a very long march - 36 miles. Some of the animals were nearly done up at the end.	

2449 Wt. W14957/M90 750,000 1/16 J.B.C. & A. Forms/C.2118/12.

Army Form C. 2118.

WAR DIARY
or
INTELLIGENCE SUMMARY
(Erase heading not required.)

Instructions regarding War Diaries and Intelligence Summaries are contained in F.S. Regs., Part II. and the Staff Manual respectively. Title Pages will be prepared in manuscript.

Place	Date	Hour	Summary of Events and Information	Remarks and references to Appendices
WARGNIES	26.2.17		Horses out in the open. Carts & harness rich. Men have good billets. Motor Transport left at 10 a.m. and arrived at WARGNIES at 5 p.m. Marching party were moved from MOYENNEVILLE by Motor lorries. Intimately a fine day; roads however very heavy. Orders received at 9 p.m. that the Bryd. was to move at 9.30 a.m. to-morrow.	
"	27.2.17		Orders received at 8.30 a.m. that the Bryd. was not move to-day. WARGNIES rich a good village but short of billets for horses. Orders received that Bryd. was now to move to-morrow starting from WARGNIES.	
"	28.2.17		The Unit moved to-day, leaving billets at 9.20 a.m. Asselling passing through the village and delayed the start somewhat. Considerable delay on the hill outside NABURS by B Echelon transport of 29 Divn. Arrived in billets (post next to) ALBERT at 8.30 a.m. a very slow march – 18 miles. Fair accommodation for men in huts — canvas roofs. Animals in the open. Hospital accommodation very limited.	

Capt: Briscoe Coy: F^d Amb:
Civ. Divn.

Serial No. 240 Medical

Confidential

War Diary

of

Sialkot Cavalry Field Ambulance

For 1.3.17

Vol XXVI

COMMITTEE FOR THE
MEDICAL HISTORY OF THE WAR
Date 6 JUL. 1917

Army Form C. 2118.

original
medical

WAR DIARY
or
INTELLIGENCE SUMMARY

(Erase heading not required.) Vol XXVI

Instructions regarding War Diaries and Intelligence Summaries are contained in F.S. Regs., Part II. and the Staff Manual respectively. Title Pages will be prepared in manuscript.

Place	Date	Hour	Summary of Events and Information	Remarks and references to Appendices
ALBERT	1.3.17		The Unit is billeted in huts just outside ALBERT on AMIENS road – moved very muddy. New Eye Refraction lately procured Sub Officer	
"	2.3.17		S.A.S Rafiuddin Khan – took one Hand Orderly and own S&T follower proceeded with a working party to form Lucknow Brigade.	
"	3.3.17		Important document for February sent to both Military Accounts. Intimation received that the Empire will arrive here to-morrow. Orders received regarding the Somme	
ST. OUEN	4.3.17		The Ambulance moved to-day leaving huts at ALBERT at 7:30 a.m – arrived in billets at ST OUEN at 1.30 a.m – about 25 miles. Ambulance cars arrived at 3 p.m. delay due to change in traffic routes. broken trunnion hemispherical Motor lorries. 29th Lancers remained at HENENCOURT.	
"	5.3.17		Billets for men fair; have standings & shelter for Hospital Accommodation limited. Received from a RMS. No 63 re. Restrictions of Motor Traffic	

J. Morris
Major IMS

Army Form C. 2118.

WAR DIARY
or
INTELLIGENCE SUMMARY

(Erase heading not required.)

Instructions regarding War Diaries and Intelligence Summaries are contained in F. S. Regs., Part II. and the Staff Manual respectively. Title Pages will be prepared in manuscript.

Place	Date	Hour	Summary of Events and Information	Remarks and references to Appendices
ST OUEN	6.3.17		Submitted a return showing notes and complaints in respect of Officers of the Unit. Sanitary arrangements complete. Deep trench latrines in use. Water from shallow wells.	
"	7.3.17		War Diary Vol XXV sent to A.D.M.S. Returns of A.S.M.S. the attest of equipment and personnel of A. Echelon of Cavalry Field Ambulance — only 3 L.C.S. Wagons present attached with A. Echelon	
"	8.3.17		Daffa. JODH SINGH — 6th Cavalry and Duffa. RAB NAWAZ KHAN — 18th Lancers reported for duty with the Unit	
"	9.3.17		One N.C.O. and two men reported as requested further in the near it is reported that the rest of division in carried on in the town	
"	10.3.17		Weather still very cold frost and snow during the week	
"	11.3.17		A.D.M.S. No 758 re disposal of personnel surrenderments	
"	12.3.17		Reported to A.D.M.S. that under new proposals he has moved to the Unit. Received from A.D.M.S. NO 777 re Instruction for disposal of surplus and Winter Stores	

WAR DIARY
or
INTELLIGENCE SUMMARY

(Erase heading not required.)

Army Form C. 2118.

Place	Date	Hour	Summary of Events and Information	Remarks and references to Appendices
S¹ OUEN	13.3.17		Kahn FEROZ KHAN and Ayar RAJE KHAN having been invalided act on struck off the strength. Sub-Assistant Surgeon AMAR CHAND proceeded to Etaples for duty. proceeding on leave to U.K. Received from a DMS No 78 9 O.R. Marking of Shell dressings. Haversacks also No 79 Sn Circular Re.	
"	14.3.17		a DMS No 786 - Regulation for destroyed damaged & unservicable clothing.	
"	15.3.17		Received from a DMS a distribution list of A & B Echelons and of 1 ack Mounted Action.	
"	16.3.17		Received a DMS No 822 re Re-innoculation of officers & men on No 829 re Jodhpur saddling of horses. Instruction issued that Unknown Bengali is to see their number distinctive dismounted movement at Bengali, 1st Qr. the situation are explained and the same may be co-related within the country may be viewed for study.	
"	17.3.17		Corp. (AN)TOO RAM, A.t. Corps arrived from the base for duty and the Unit. A DMS No 849 re Self-inflicted injuries.	

2449 Wt. W14957/M90 750,000 1/16 J.B.C. & A. Forms/C.2118/12.

Army Form C. 2118.

WAR DIARY
or
INTELLIGENCE SUMMARY

(Erase heading not required.)

Instructions regarding War Diaries and Intelligence Summaries are contained in F. S. Regs., Part II. and the Staff Manual respectively. Title Pages will be prepared in manuscript.

Place	Date	Hour	Summary of Events and Information	Remarks and references to Appendices
ST OUEN	17.3.17		Received Orders at 12.20 p.m. that the Brigade would proceed at 2.30 p.m. to proceed via Villers hocher to proceed to BOUZINCOURT. The Ambulance left at 2.30 p.m. - proceeded via VIGNACOURT and TREMAS to ALBERT and bivouacked for the night at AVELUY - arrived at 11.30 p.m. Rang the S.O.C. of the brigade at 11.0 p.m. re operations for next day. Received orders at 12.0 a.m. re movement forward. Is believed to remain in huts but detached Field Ambulance Section - taken over by proposed ride to 3 Wood Collieries and one agger sent in their places. Capt Newcomen in charge. On march to-day men stout 30 miles the remainder movement conveyed in lorries.	
AVELUY	18.3.17		The Brigade Supply Dump - moved off at 5.30 a.m. to proceed forward at 6.30 a.m. The Capt. Mitchell decided profound the Brigade - the Mission charge reported to Brigade Major. The Ambulance marched up to A Chelen - B Chelen and Main Ambulance remained at AVELUY	

WAR DIARY
or
INTELLIGENCE SUMMARY

Army Form C. 2118.

Place	Date	Hour	Summary of Events and Information	Remarks and references to Appendices
AVELUY	18-3-17		The A Echelon of the Ambulances consisted of 3 L.G.S. Wagons 3 L.H. Ambulances and 2 Water Carts. The column arrived at MIRAMONT at about 11 a.m. Roads very bad. NIRAMONT a heap of ruins. The column improved past onth of MIRAMONT for the night. A.D.M.S. N⁰ 851 sr. the direct of Dental Cases and N⁰ 851 sr. Detached Units reports	
ACHIET LE GRAND	19-3-17		Received orders at 8 a.m. that the Unit would move to LE SARS moved through MIRAMONT at 9:30 a.m. and proceeded to GRANDCOURT to draw rations returned as far as MIRAMONT and then on to COURCELETTE roads very bad and we had great difficulty in getting along. Considerable delay on path on the main road. On arrival at LE SARS received orders to go on to ACHIET LE GRAND. Should have been nearer rations at LE SARS but were not allowed to stop on the road and had to remain on without them. Found the road to GREVILLERS impassable and eventually got down the railway line and came in to road to Achiet	M

Army Form C. 2118.

WAR DIARY
or
INTELLIGENCE SUMMARY

(Erase heading not required.)

Instructions regarding War Diaries and Intelligence Summaries are contained in F. S. Regs., Part II. and the Staff Manual respectively. Title Pages will be prepared in manuscript.

Place	Date	Hour	Summary of Events and Information	Remarks and references to Appendices
ACHIET LE GRAND	19.3.17		Arrived in ACHIET at about 1 am - halted throughout in a field. Very little cover left in the village. Moving of the previous day had though up. Mounted Pair Camp in about 4.50 am & continued all night. Capt. Luion came in and reported that the Pack Mounted Section were established at ERVILLERS and were working forward from there. Farm patrols had been in action & a few wounded brought in.	
BIHUCOURT	20.3.17		Could find no suitable place for an HQrs Survey established in ACHIET, proceeded to BIHUCOURT - I had started and arrived just ahead. O.P. detachment of No.56 F. Ambulance to occupy part of the factory and received wounded there. Staff Captain of the 18th and my own had already been established. A Echelon of the Ghost moved on to BIHUCOURT at 10.30 a.m. On L.H. Ambulance sent up to ERVILLERS for evacuation of wounded to BIHUCOURT Regt Room awarded in neighbourhood. One coy awarded & one awarded back to No.56 F. Amb at IRLES in the morning.	Nil

2449 Wt. W14957/M90 750,000 1/16 J.B.C. & A. Forms/C.2118/12.

Army Form C. 2118.

WAR DIARY
or
INTELLIGENCE SUMMARY
(Erase heading not required.)

Place	Date	Hour	Summary of Events and Information	Remarks and references to Appendices
BIHUCOURT	20.3.17		British and Indian wounded received during the day. Attention was now directed all had been removed. Enemy however very lively throughout evening & also very numerous. Two Indians who had died of wounds during the night were buried near the Hospital.	JM
	21.3.17		Forwarded cars to N° 56 F. Ambulance at IRLES, to see Runner Station & N° 56 F. Amb. moved back BIHUES during the morning. Proceeded to ERVILLERS to see S.O.C. of the Bde, arranged that the Ambulance would delay for 151/4th COURT when there was better accommodation for wounded. From the 24th Mountain Ambulance got ERVILLERS thither from accommodation for wounded Infantry men of outposts observed at rest. La R.H. position has shown some good work: all the wounded reported have been transferred Evacuation 8 wounded from A.D.S. went to B.M.O.L.t. Amb. at BUCQUOY - road in forward for hire Ambulances. Indirect from well on the Factory yard.	JM

2449 Wt W14957/Mg0 750,000 1/16 J.B.C. & A. Forms/C.2118/12.

Army Form C. 2118.

WAR DIARY
or
INTELLIGENCE SUMMARY

(Erase heading not required.)

Place	Date	Hour	Summary of Events and Information	Remarks and references to Appendices
BIHUCOURT	22.3.17		Inspected arms and ammunition of N°1 & 2 Coys at BUCQUOY. Fine weather but very cold	J.H.
	23.3.17		Inspected roads through HAMELET LE PETIT MIRAISIEUX found impassable at present. Reported the Company were employed extra to practice. Have inspected such as roads on the right. S.S. DENT evacuated with a cough. If this caught a Rifle Indisposable. NMS reported from Mefy & Capt. H. Thoresback. Saw MS Eden are approved from Duty, met Lieut. B. at Sole Premier Battalion	J.H.
	24.3.17		Proceeded to ERVILLERS to see O.M. Easton to try to arrange to use 2 days of mty's for such time bore through to as to keep reported from Premier Battalion as weak for.	J.H.
	25.3.17		Received orders late at night that the Company moves to join more truck to IRLES to-morrow morning	J.H.

WAR DIARY
or
INTELLIGENCE SUMMARY

(Erase heading not required.)

Army Form C. 2118.

Place	Date	Hour	Summary of Events and Information	Remarks and references to Appendices
IRLES	26.3.17		Pom sick evacuated to BUCQUOY. The Ambulance left BIHUCOURT at 9.30 a.m and proceeded via GREVILLERS-IRLES arrived about noon. Raining all the morning - roads very and had some difficulty in getting round. Evacuated system. Company faced South of IRLES. Tents did not arrive till nearly dark. Arranged for evacuation of sick through No.1 M.L. Field Ambulance. The P.M. section opened just before the Sunset. Left BIHUCOURT	
"	27.3.17		Visited Brigade H.Q. Weather still very bad. A.D.M.S.M.O. 903 re "Memo on Espinoy"	
"	28.3.17		Medical Board to examine Lieut. Howston 19 Pioneers for commission in Indian Army. A.D.M.S. 2nd Cav. Division received the Cert. Lieut. Simon Pamic to be Temp. Capt. dated 11.3.17 A.D.M.S. No 1028 re Care of effects of Sick + Wounded Officers. Returned 10 msgs to A.D.M.S.	
"	29.3.17		Very bad weather again. Intimation received that the Unit will move to N.J of IRLES to-morrow morning.	

2449 Wt. W14957/M90 750,000 1/16 J.B.C. & A. Forms/C.2118/12.

Medical
Serial No. 240

Confidential

War Diary

of

51st M.A.   C.F.A.

From 1.4.17.   to 30.4.17

Vol XXVII

COMMITTEE FOR THE
MEDICAL HISTORY OF THE WAR
Date 6 JUL. 1917

Original

Army Form C. 2118.

Original
Medical

WAR DIARY
or
INTELLIGENCE SUMMARY

(Erase heading not required.) Vol. XXVII

Instructions regarding War Diaries and Intelligence Summaries are contained in F. S. Regs., Part II. and the Staff Manual respectively. Title Pages will be prepared in manuscript.

Place	Date	Hour	Summary of Events and Information	Remarks and references to Appendices
IRLES	1.4.17		Three Armourers and Saddlers Hotho sent to D.A.C. 3rd Division	
"	2.4.17		No 7291,872 Driver HEALEY L.D.C.H.T. and N.T.29,379 Driver Cooper D.A.C. A.D.C.H.T. arrived from the Base for duty with this Unit. Received A.O.M.S. N. 1160 re Smallpox Epidemic	nil
"	3.4.17		War Diary Vol XXVI sent to A.D.M.S. Since yesterday midday the weather has been very severe – accompanied by strong North-Easterly wind in the afternoon which was within the scenes and made sleeping difficult. From shells, field has been destroyed. The camp in which the team was can be found.	nil
"	4.4.17		Weather still bad. One L.D. Horse died this morning from hurts. Effects field.	nil
"	5.4.17		Intimation received that the Brigade will move sometime tomorrow. Cook Sergt Belk of A.H. Corps evacuated sick to hospital to day. One L.D. Mule suffering from Stomatitis had to be destroyed	nil
BIHUCOURT	6.4.17		Driver Hawkins returned from Hospital to day. The Ambulance Moved at 5 pm Beings ordered BIHUCOURT	

Army Form C. 2118.

WAR DIARY
or
INTELLIGENCE SUMMARY
(Erase heading not required.)

Place	Date	Hour	Summary of Events and Information	Remarks and references to Appendices
BIHUCOURT	6.4.17		Arrived in camp at 4 p.m. Roads very heavy. Shelter had again this evening.	
	7.4.17		Two Sections A B C up evacuated sick without any cases	
	8.4.17		Two Motor Ambulances reported to tent subdivided journey Brancria and B Section when A Section was short. Pack Mounted Section ordered in dismounted as stretcher bearers. A report on the working of the Pack Mounted section was given to A.D.M.S. Two motor ambulances today very cold.	
	9.4.17		Two Ford cars received in exchange for two Ambulance cars. Lt? Mr. Davidson and Mr. Kerr?? A.B.M.T. made a trip in the 7th Field Brigade order and that struck up a train?? proceeded with the ??. Northern rain has come down rain most of the day & night	

Army Form C. 2118.

WAR DIARY
or
INTELLIGENCE SUMMARY

(Erase heading not required.)

Place	Date	Hour	Summary of Events and Information	Remarks and references to Appendices
BIHUCOURT	10.4.17		Brigade and A echelon moved off at 2.0 am. This morning proceeding via SAPIGNIES to neighbourhood of MORY. Leading men halted behind SAPIGNIES and remained there till 6.30 am. 6.30 am heavy snow at dawn delayed digging in to camp. Snow most of the day. Orders received at the Bivouac and moved out at 2.30 am to shelters & billets to follow later	
	11.4.17		R.M. Ruden under Capt Hawkinson and Mackness a.m. to join Rachet Brigade. A Echelon of the Ambulance left 7 am from SAPIGNIES As Echelon proceeded via many to MORY. My very bad. The Ambulance were billeted outside the village or the Echelon there held up for the or. It was reported that there had been many casualties in Rackett Brigade - particularly the 17th Lancers. Bare Brown under Capt Green and D.A.D. Rajindah Khan sent across country to render medical aid. 3 L.H. Ambulance Major ...	

2449 Wt. W14957/M90 750,000 1/16 J.B.C. & A. Forms/C.2118/12.

WAR DIARY
INTELLIGENCE SUMMARY

Army Form C. 2118.

Place	Date	Hour	Summary of Events and Information	Remarks and references to Appendices
BIHUCOURT	11/4/17		Got ready and sent to B70 2/2 W.R. Regt Ambulance at the [?] hurriedly fixed from five [?] not OC Regt sent [?] for all casualties from 2nd Cavalry Brigade Regt though his Ambulance. Recd a message of arrival of ambulances Capt. [?] came later to say they can [?]. All wounded had been [?] by deputy Sergeant & say that these men sent few casualties on the 4 Canada. [?] Been [?] returned to HQ & the [?] of 2 & 2 ambulance [?]. Major Kingston & 2/3 [?] at 8 [?] [?]. Return to Camp [?] near BAPAUME. Leave camp as we [?] many MO [?] having [?] arrived at 7.30 p.m. [?] section and marching party [?] [?]	
"	12.4.17		Reorganism after night's long call. No drills and men are [?] cleaning the night from out experience.	

Army Form C. 2118.

WAR DIARY or INTELLIGENCE SUMMARY

(Erase heading not required.)

Place	Date	Hour	Summary of Events and Information	Remarks and references to Appendices
BIHUCOURT	13.4.17		Better weather but still very cold	
AVELUY	14.4.17		The Ambulance moved with the Brigade to AVELUY, left at 11 a.m. and proceeded part of the way down very bad roads. Heavy frogs and had some difficulty in getting S.O. wagons along. From IRLES to AVELUY very bad. Arrived at 5 pm. Weather particularly bad and very distressing. Warm	
"	15.4.17		The Unit in ambulances huts ex tents AVELUY became very busy. Knees under cover - incomplete. Camp very dirty. Bad weather again. Rain all day	
"	16.4.17		Orders re-published regarding prevention of Trench fever. Sanitary arrangements completed. Honneimann hut disposed of to incinerator.	
"	17.4.17		Arranged with Sanitary Officer for new baths in ALBERT. Still bad weather. AAMS No 1892 re Scabies Report	

2449 Wt. W14957/M90 750,000 1/16 J.B.C. & A. Forms/C.2118/12.

WAR DIARY
INTELLIGENCE SUMMARY

Army Form C. 2118.

Place	Date	Hour	Summary of Events and Information	Remarks and references to Appendices
AVELUY	18.4.17		Seven days recent operations all the command have had an extra issue owing to the severe weather many of them particularly the L.D. Horses and D. & T. horses have had addition in addition the civilians & animals which render it especially severe. About the 15.0 inst. letter extra food was issued could not be supplied to the animals.	
"	19.4.17		Animals received to be duty and from in addition fully	
"	20.4.17		Received A.D.M.S. No. 141 re Road Repair	
"	21.4.17		Weather better but still very cold	
"	22.4.17			
"	23.4.17		Received A.D.M.S No 149 re totals of Transport and W.T 3 cc Para of Enemy Origin	
"	24.4.17		Order to D.I Knox invalided out to Blighty left Section	
COISY	25.4.17		Det. Unit moved today to COISY left at Section fully equipped to Establishment including 16 cart. eys.	

2449 Wt. W14957/M90 750,000 1/16 J.B.C. & A. Forms/C.2118/12.

WAR DIARY
or
INTELLIGENCE SUMMARY

Army Form C. 2118.

Place	Date	Hour	Summary of Events and Information	Remarks and references to Appendices
COUIN	26.4.17		The Ambulance is now located in huts just behind COUIN. Huts fair but rather dark. Have emergency established in hospital Bidet and Indian tents on own. In other infectious cases. There are now a sewing company & heat station system in full swing and hope sanitation fair. Latrines buckets in use and contents removed by local lorries for incineration. Camp fairly clean when taken over. Inspected water carts.	
	27.4.17		Sanitary arrangements completed. Horses now properly covered. Huts	
	28.4.17		Received A.D.M.S. No 1595 re Discipline. Attempted & sent reply. Convoy to divn.	
	29.4.17		Reported to Brigade H.Q. condition of camp & huts when taken over.	
	30.4.17		Received A.D.M.S. No 1641 re Burial of Indians	

Comdg: Sanitary Coy. F⁴ Amb.
A.D. Cav. Divⁿ

Army Form C. 2118.

WAR DIARY
or
INTELLIGENCE SUMMARY
(Erase heading not required.)

Instructions regarding War Diaries and Intelligence Summaries are contained in F.S. Regs., Part II. and the Staff Manual respectively. Title Pages will be prepared in manuscript.

Place	Date	Hour	Summary of Events and Information	Remarks and references to Appendices
IRLES	29.3.17		Bletchley of the Unit reported from AVELUY this afternoon. Remainder of Unit Q.O.M.S. No. 1041 6 w. Show Originals	
"	30.3.17		Oh moves to other end of village was cancelled & night duty had been started & act up to recce ground for Symptom Refinements than any. On Wired Chapels and on St Theodoras reported from outlayer outposts at Shownmentoned even	
"	31.3.17		Pub: Movement Say tower closed reported from boar to U.K. Weather still very bad. – cold & wet – A.O.M.S. No. 1125 &c. Standisation of Master	

Com^e: Statoute Cav: F^d Amb
Cav: Divis^l

Original

Medical

Serial No: 240.

Confidential

War Diary

of

No 5 Cavalry Field Ambulance Sialkote

from 1st May to 30th June 1917.

Vol XXVIII

COMMITTEE FOR THE
MEDICAL HISTORY OF THE WAR
Date 27 JUL. 1917

Army Form C. 2118.

Original

WAR DIARY
or
INTELLIGENCE SUMMARY

Military

(Erase heading not required.) VOL XXVIII

Instructions regarding War Diaries and Intelligence
Summaries are contained in F. S. Regs., Part II.
and the Staff Manual respectively. Title Pages
will be prepared in manuscript.

Place	Date	Hour	Summary of Events and Information	Remarks and references to Appendices
COUIN	1.5.17		Received A.T.M.S No 1655 re Carriage of Wives hole-ex-published here allowance taken up to force of the titled up.	
	2.5.17		Received ca TMS No 670 re 4 hours statements and No 1672 re hooting of patients. Proceeded to office of AMS 48th army A.T.M.S 1 this Division	
	3.5.17		One Cook and one Servant proceeded to Conference that 58th Stationary Hospital. Freed up journeyed. First Clearing No 24 No 70 Brown Wood also No 47 arrived from Fr. for duty with the Unit. Received circular re Sophora Bye fuschia	
	4.5.17		Cash account for April sent to Cont. Military Accounts. Only Cpl inspected 11 clerks thown 5th A. Echelon no movement to station 7th Brigade this morning.	
	5.5.17		War Diary XXVII sent to AMD. Received from army No 1750 re Carriage of Iron rations	
	6.5.17		Received from army No 1737 re Carriage & Forwarding of Baggage.	

Army Form C. 2118.

WAR DIARY
or
INTELLIGENCE SUMMARY

(Erase heading not required.)

Instructions regarding War Diaries and Intelligence Summaries are contained in F. S. Regs., Part II. and the Staff Manual respectively. Title Pages will be prepared in manuscript.

Place	Date	Hour	Summary of Events and Information	Remarks and references to Appendices
COBIN	7.5.19		One Ward totally prepared for temporary stay of N.Z. Stationary Hospital	
"	8.5.19		Orders re Typhus out republished	
"	9.5.19		Lieut. Morgan I.M.S. detailed to proceed to N.O. Surreysur- rampur	
"	10.5.19		One Ward ready and two patients received from day at 11 h. St. Hospital	
"	11.5.19			
"	12.5.19			
"	13.5.19		Order re Control of dogs republished. One Ward closed and the Wards prepared for study with the Chief. Two brown mules with 40 Indian personnel under P.O. Keppeldin Khan prevailed here and dismounted men for transport to new area	
"	14.5.19		On been evacuated etc. Intimation received that the impending move to new area on 15th inst. Orders issued regarding the same	

2449 Wt. W14957/M90 750,000 1/16 J.B.C. & A. Forms/C.2118/12.

Army Form C. 2118.

WAR DIARY or INTELLIGENCE SUMMARY

(Erase heading not required.)

Place	Date	Hour	Summary of Events and Information	Remarks and references to Appendices
VILLE SOUS CORBIE	15.5.17		The Unit arrived to-day - marching 1st Dukhak Brigade left Blais at 8.30 a.m. Unit did not H.Q. Echelon accompanying them. Echelon arrived at Ville at 4 p.m. Fatigue party arrived for the night from the river. Fatigue party left to clear up ground at billets and in camp vacated from the Unit.	
MAUREPAS	16.5.17		The Unit arrived with the Brigade this morning at 9 an arrived at 3 p.m. Accommodation in huts. Weather dry some slight rain.	
FOURQUES	17.5.17		The Unit moved this morning and reached the new area at 5 p.m. Fine weather.	
"	18.5.17		Orders received with supplies and Capt. Matson's presence, Accommodation (huts + tents) and all transport at 5 tents received from Brigade for movement.	
"	19.5.17		Remedy arrangement completed deep truck to lower area.	
"	20.5.17		Pte Warren M.T. reported from C.O. was placed in Sergt of Horses	

Army Form C. 2118.

WAR DIARY
or
INTELLIGENCE SUMMARY
(Erase heading not required.)

Instructions regarding War Diaries and Intelligence Summaries are contained in F. S. Regs., Part II. and the Staff Manual respectively. Title Pages will be prepared in manuscript.

Place	Date	Hour	Summary of Events and Information	Remarks and references to Appendices
FOURQUES	21.5.17			
"	22.5.17		Capt-Quar RSMcO rejoined from leave. Escadron A Neil rejoined	
			At Cavalry Corps	
"	23.5.17		—	
"	24.5.17		3 Kiens A&S Cops detached for duty at Dieppe	
"	25.5.17		Monthly Report for the month sent to ADMS	
"	26.5.17		S.R.O No 257 re damage to Corps commanded workshops	
"	27.5.17		Received ADMS No 257 re "Rebuilt staff and No 287 re Convoy of Mules in Parks	
"	28.5.17		On L D Mule succeeded to let Rievere on next to senior to Ordnance Workshop. Rare medical equipment returned to T.O. Supply Column	
"	29.5.17		Order re Buildings received in the village received	Nil

Army Form C. 2118.

WAR DIARY
or
INTELLIGENCE SUMMARY
(Erase heading not required.)

Instructions regarding War Diaries and Intelligence Summaries are contained in F. S. Regs., Part II. and the Staff Manual respectively. Title Pages will be prepared in manuscript.

Place	Date	Hour	Summary of Events and Information	Remarks and references to Appendices
FOURQUES	30.5.19		Received A&MS N°2231 in Vehicles Medical Motor Units and N°2216 in Vehicles Motor Pedicular on admission	
	31.5.19		Draw Work HT evacuated sick Details moved to proceed for duty at Main Anvers Station 14 & 5 Composcience	

Com: Sialcote Cav: F^d Amb:
4 ^th Cav: Divis^n:

2449 Wt. W14957/M90 750,000 1/16 J.B.C. & A. Forms/C.2118/12.

Medical

Confidential

War Diary

of

2nd/1st Lowland Field Ambulance

From 1.6.17 to 30.6.17

Vol. XXIX

Original

Original

Army Form C. 2118.
Medical

WAR DIARY
or
INTELLIGENCE SUMMARY

(Erase heading not required.) Vol XXIX

Instructions regarding War Diaries and Intelligence Summaries are contained in F.S. Regs., Part II. and the Staff Manual respectively. Title Pages will be prepared in manuscript.

Place	Date	Hour	Summary of Events and Information	Remarks and references to Appendices
FOURQUES	1.6.17		One Water Cart sent-in-loan - to Mhow Brigade H.Qrs. Received ADMS N° 2272 re "Greasing"	RW
"	2.6.17		Cook evacuated to May recd to Col. Mullay. Received 1.E.F.A. War Diary Vol XXVIII forwarded to A.D.M.S. Subaltern received at this Unit and a detachment for duty at the Main Dressing Station - Recensidered C.F.A. ADSMS Cavalry Corps reverted to duty	RW
"	3.6.17		Two Officers and 110 British and Indian personnel received for duty at Main Dressing Station. Received ADMS N° 2326 re "Water Carts"	RW
"	4.6.17		N° 74/239 506 Farrier Rimmoor arrived for duty with the Unit	RW
"	5.6.17		Received ADMS N° 2572 re "Discovery of Prisoners"	RW
"	6.6.17		—	
"	7.6.17		Received ADMS N° 2613 re "Slag Roads". Communicated to all personnel of the Unit. One Bearer AB Cox evacuated sick	RW
"	8.6.17		Pnn. Woods evacuated sick re attack of the Lungs. Received ADMS N° 2460 re "Cleanliness of Water Carts"	W. Moore Major RAMC

2449 Wt. W14957/M90 750,000 1/16 J.B.C. & A. Forms/C.2118/12.

Army Form C. 2118.

WAR DIARY
or
INTELLIGENCE SUMMARY

(Erase heading not required.)

Instructions regarding War Diaries and Intelligence Summaries are contained in F. S. Regs., Part II. and the Staff Manual respectively. Title Pages will be prepared in manuscript.

Place	Date	Hour	Summary of Events and Information	Remarks and references to Appendices
FOURQUES	9.6.17		Bann T SaxH, A.B. Corps evacuated sick to church 19th Chargth	JM
	10.6.17		Received ASMs No 2466 in "Percentage of Inoculations"	JM
	11.6.17		- - - - - -	
	12.6.17		Received ASMs No 2532 in "Surging" and No 2502 in "Treatment of Wounds"	JM
	13.6.17		- - - - - -	
	14.6.17		- - - - - -	
	15.6.17		Visit from the Catering Officer. Corn magful hints on cooking. Change of diet - re Received ASMs No 2972 re "Trench Fever"	JM
	16.6.17		Corporal Wheeler sent to Divisional 4 Or for duty at the workshop	JM
	17.6.17		Pte Thompson proceeded on one months leave to UK. Issued orders in dispatch of beans and unhulled Kitchen carriers for Emergency Ben Vants	JM

2449 Wt. W14957/M90 750,000 1/16 J.B.C. & A. Forms/C.2118/12.

Army Form C. 2118.

WAR DIARY
or
INTELLIGENCE SUMMARY

(Erase heading not required.)

Instructions regarding War Diaries and Intelligence Summaries are contained in F. S. Regs., Part II. and the Staff Manual respectively. Title Pages will be prepared in manuscript.

Place	Date	Hour	Summary of Events and Information	Remarks and references to Appendices
FOURDREB	18.6.17		One L.D. Mule died last night. Strength N° 74/05732. D° Cavalry. One O.R. reported for duty and the Chief B.S.M.S. Cavalry Corps hospitalled the Unit this morning.	
"	19.6.17		Received A.D.M.S. N° 2559 re Executive Org of Mule Vehicles - communicated to all M.T.	
"	20.6.17		Pte Pulish Raine proceeded for duty at Main Dressing Station. Reinstated CFA Received A.D.M.S. N°2653 re Dysentery Cases.	
"	21.6.17		3 L.D. Mules received from the base. General instr. th Day circulated	
"	22.6.17		Received A.D.M.S. N° 2747 re Burial of Manure.	
"	23.6.17		Driver Kelly A/C L.H.T. rejoined from hospital. Received A.D.M.S. N° 2775 re Necessity of Inoculation	

WAR DIARY or INTELLIGENCE SUMMARY

Army Form C. 2118.

Place	Date	Hour	Summary of Events and Information	Remarks and references to Appendices
FOUR QUES	24.6.17		Pte Pennington R.A.M.C. transferred to Officer i/c A.T.M.S. struck off the strength. Orders Traffic Routes issued to M.T.	JM
	25.6.17		Received A.T.M.S. No 2821 re Horse Respirators	JM
	26.6.17		—	
	27.6.17		3 Horses A.S. Corps arrived from Kanu for Unit with the Unit	JM
	28.6.17		Received A.T.M.S No 2881 re Missing of runaway Wounded	JM
	29.6.17		—	
	30.6.17		One Horse – Runaway Nadhu – transferred to Remounted CFA. One Horse – Ram Din – arrived from remounted CFA to Unit, with this Unit. Orders received for despatch of Emergency Reserve Parts	

J Munro T.M.S.

Com: Sialkote Cav: 1st Ind:
4. Cav: Divn:

W. medical

Serial No: 240.

[Stamp: COMMITTEE FOR THE MEDICAL HISTORY OF THE WAR
Date 16 OCT 1917]

Confidential

War Diary
of
2nd Nat. Cavalry Field Ambulance.

From 1.7.17.
To 31.7.17.

Vol. XXX

original
July 1917

Army Form C. 2118.

WAR DIARY
or
INTELLIGENCE SUMMARY

(Erase heading not required.)

Vol XXX

Place	Date	Hour	Summary of Events and Information	Remarks and references to Appendices
FOURQUES	1.7.17		Re Emergency Kneeparty – 16 Bearers sent to another carriages – proceeded to report to O.C. Judhpur C.F.A. Received A.D.M.S. No 2954, re "Carriage of Bar Rations." Imprest Account for June sent to Cont: Military Accts. War Diary Vol XXIX forwarded to A.D.M.S.	JM
"	2.7.17		– – – –	
"	3.7.17		Emergency Bearer Party reported early this morning. Received A.D.M.S No 2977 re "Months of Vernacular."	JM
"	4.7.17		Orr Bearer Ramdhar- evacuated sick. Received A.D.M.S. No 3014 re Lascars.	JM
"	5.7.17		– – – –	
"	6.7.17		Received from O.C. A.S.C. Circular No 66 to 77.	JM
"	7.7.17		Received from A.D.M.S. No M.3097 re "Returns and Instructions for dealing with flies and vermin"	JM Major I/MS

2449 Wt. W14957/M90 750,000 1/16 J.B.C. & A: Forms/C.2118/12.

Army Form C. 2118.

WAR DIARY
or
INTELLIGENCE SUMMARY

(Erase heading not required.)

Instructions regarding War Diaries and Intelligence Summaries are contained in F. S. Regs., Part II. and the Staff Manual respectively. Title Pages will be prepared in manuscript.

Place	Date	Hour	Summary of Events and Information	Remarks and references to Appendices
FOURAVES	8-7-17		No 6105 Pte NORRIS ROWE arrived for duty with the Unit	JW
"	9.7.17		Bad weather with much rain during last 2 days	JW
"	10.7.17		Detachment doing duty with 15th Unit this morning. Received A.F.W.S No 3160 re "Recent Enemy Gas Bombardment".	JW
"	11.7.17		Received from A.F.W.S No 3186 re Trench Control and Road Discipline and No 3193 re A & D Books	JW
"	12.7.17		Received from O.C. Recuperated C.F.A re commendation of the work done by the detachment of this Unit – while with the Main Dressing Station – Published in the Order Book	JW
"	13.7.17		Water sterilization tablets issued. Under instructions from Divisional H.Q. 4 Rainy River men to-day handed over to Pulbut Brigade H.Q. This leave the Unit with Thorius – 30) Murr Murr, ? no. casuals and H. Noraes	JW

2449 Wt. W14957/Mgo 759,000 1/16 J.B.C. & A. Forms/C.2118/12.

Army Form C. 2118.

WAR DIARY
or
INTELLIGENCE SUMMARY
(Erase heading not required.)

Instructions regarding War Diaries and Intelligence Summaries are contained in F. S. Regs., Part II. and the Staff Manual respectively. Title Pages will be prepared in manuscript.

Place	Date	Hour	Summary of Events and Information	Remarks and references to Appendices
FOURQUES	13.7.17		The Path Mounted Section ordered down ratio 11 Rating animals and 3 Pack animals. with a total war of nco, 11 riding animals the number available for the Pack Mounted section used to only 7 n. 8. Two Mouted Orderlies detached for temporary duty with Labour Companies	Sgd
"	14.7.17		Received from A/SMS No 3253 re Contacts Jaudis opened cases	Sgd
"	15.7.17	7	A.D. Horses received from Base – 40	Sgd
"	16.7.17		Lieut Kalapienwalla proceeded on leave to U.K. Ordered that the Motor Cars will be inspected daily	Sgd
"	17.7.17		Third Army Cir. Memo No 392 re Discipline-Saluting - read out on parade.	Sgd
"	18.7.17			

WAR DIARY
or
INTELLIGENCE SUMMARY

(Erase heading not required.)

Army Form C. 2118.

Place	Date	Hour	Summary of Events and Information	Remarks and references to Appendices
FOURAGES	19.7.17		Received A.S.M.S No. 33329 re Sap Ration	AH
"	20.7.17		Capt. Hawkins proceeded on leave to U.K. 3 horses recently cast by Boards of Remounts evacuated to Avesnes. M.V.B	AH
"	21.7.17		Received A.S.M.S No. 33510 re Disposal of effects of deceased	AH
"	22.7.17		Received A.S.M.S No. 3271 re Promotion of Officers	AH
"	23.7.17		- - - - -	
"	24.7.17		Three A.V.C men of the Unit proceeded on leave to U.K.	AH
"	25.7.17		- - - - -	
"	26.7.17		Received from A.S.M.S No. 35115 re Census of Horses & Mules Regimental & Mounted men. Very successful horse show on the terrain during last 2 days. Received announcement D Army Ord.	AH

Army Form C. 2118.

1st Series

WAR DIARY
or
INTELLIGENCE SUMMARY
(Erase heading not required.)

Instructions regarding War Diaries and Intelligence Summaries are contained in F.S. Regs., Part II. and the Staff Manual respectively. Title Pages will be prepared in manuscript.

Original

Place	Date	Hour	Summary of Events and Information	Remarks and references to Appendices
FOURQUES	27.7.17		Received from A.D.M.S. Memo re "San Pearing" Manadores against Flu	
"	28.7.17		Received from A.D.M.S. No M/5637 re Measures against Flu	
"	29.7.17		Lieut Valspinewill returned from leave 5.P.M. Received from A.D.M.S. No M/3465 re Use of Flavine	
"	30.7.17		Received from A.D.M.S. No 3468 Report of San Cases. Weather inclement lately. Fair amount of rain	
"	31.7.17		Driver Keelan a/c 1.7. evacuated sick	

J. Moorin
Major I.M.S.
Lieut: Sialcote Cav: F.R. Amb
1/1 Cav: Division

Original

Medical

Serial No. 240.

Confidential

War Diary
of
2nd Kut Cavalry Field Ambulance

From 1.8.17.
To 31.8.17.

Aug 1917

(Vol XXXI)

COMMITTEE FOR THE
MEDICAL HISTORY OF THE WAR
Date 16 OCT. 1917

Army Form C. 2118.
Medical

Original

WAR DIARY
or
INTELLIGENCE SUMMARY

(Erase heading not required.)

Vol. XXXI

Instructions regarding War Diaries and Intelligence Summaries are contained in F.S. Regs., Part II. and the Staff Manual respectively. Title Pages will be prepared in manuscript.

[FIELD AMBULANCE SIALKOTE stamp]

Place	Date	Hour	Summary of Events and Information	Remarks and references to Appendices
FOURQUES	1.8.17		Acquittance rolls and cash account for July sent to Cont. Mil. Auds. I.E.F.F. War diary for July (Vol. XXX) forwarded to A.D.M.S. Received Circular No. SS/175 re "Notes on use of Anazak"	
"	2.8.17			
"	3.8.17		---	
"	4.8.17		Two L.D. Mules received from the base. Received A.S.M.S. No 357 re "Effect of new type of Gas Shell" attention of all M.Os drawn to A.S.M.S. No 104/3578. Cases of Poisoning	
"	5.8.17		No T/3/92 Pte Cooke and No T/306253 Dr Kemble received as reinforcements from the base. Received A.S.M.S. No 104/3578 re X-Ray Examinations. Also R.A.M.C. Corps Orders	
ST OMER	6.8.17		The Unit moved to ST OMER this morning and took over the Divisional Rest Station from Lucknow C.F.A. including tents & stores. Handed over 13 tents to O.C. Ambala C.F.A at FOURQUES. Received Special Order of the Day	

Corps: Sialcote Cav. F'ld Amb.

WAR DIARY
or
INTELLIGENCE SUMMARY

(Erase heading not required.)

Army Form C. 2118.

Place	Date	Hour	Summary of Events and Information	Remarks and references to Appendices
ST CREN	7.8.17		Additional Hospital Standing Orders published	
"	8.8.17		Received AFM'S No M/3651 re Weekly Inspection for Scabies	
			Dormitory arrangements improved	
"	9.8.17		Kit, tents and stores outside regular equipment sent to A.O.M.S. 3 Bearers reported from duty at Div. H.Q.	
			Received AFM'S No 3683 re Treatment of Temporary Teachers	
"	10.8.17		Orders regarding precautions against flies published	
			Received AFM'S No M/3700 re Treatment of Ear Cases	
"	11.8.17		Sgt. Hill A.O.M.T. attended Ear Course. Received AFM'S	
			No M/3707 re Drawing of Medical Stores	
"	12.8.17		Received AFM'S No 3727 "New German Gas" and No 3725 re	
			Manner required of Medical Services	
"	13.8.17		Received Brig. Orders re Defence against Gas and communicated to all personnel	
	14.8.17			

Army Form C. 2118.

WAR DIARY
or
INTELLIGENCE SUMMARY
(Erase heading not required.)

Instructions regarding War Diaries and Intelligence Summaries are contained in F. S. Regs., Part II. and the Staff Manual respectively. Title Pages will be prepared in manuscript.

Place	Date	Hour	Summary of Events and Information	Remarks and references to Appendices
ST CREN	15.8.17		Received ADMS No M/3761 re Meaning and No M/3767 re Mustard Gas Poisoning.	JW
	16.8.17		Received from Cavalry Corps Circular No M/34/10 G/177.17 re "Gas Exposure in men at C.C. Stations"	JW
	17.8.17		—	
	18.8.17		Received ADMS No M/3819 re "Procedure for evacuating Wounded Cases"	JW
	19.8.17		2nd Lieut. Hurst U.S.A.M.S. arrived for duty with this Unit on leave of Lieut. Narayan I.M.S. Received ADMS No M/3856 re "System of dealing with Scout Patrols". Lieut. Narayan I.M.S. re reported his departure for duty with 36th Labour Troops - under AD MS VI Corps. Ordered that in future P.H. Returns for Regiments not always be corrected in this area. Received ADMS No M/3862 re Regiment of Wounded Cases.	JW
	20.8.17			JW

Army Form C. 2118.

WAR DIARY
or
INTELLIGENCE SUMMARY
(Erase heading not required.)

Instructions regarding War Diaries and Intelligence Summaries are contained in F.S. Regs., Part II. and the Staff Manual respectively. Title Pages will be prepared in manuscript.

Place	Date	Hour	Summary of Events and Information	Remarks and references to Appendices
ST EBEN	21.8.17		S.R.O. No 2529 read out to parade. Ball M.T. personnel.	JH
"	22.8.17		Capt Lewin R.A.M.C. proceeded to-day for temporary duty with A.D.S. of 10th F. Ambulance. Pte Beaven A.S.C. and one Studts arrived for duty with the Unit.	JH
"	23.8.17		"	JH
"	24.8.17		Received A.O.Mds No M/3916 re San Antonio	JH
"	25.8.17		Received A.O.Mds No M/3917 re Enumeration of persons	JH
"	26.8.17			
"	27.8.17		Special Order of the Day circulated	JH
"	28.8.17		Received A.O.Mds No M/3998 re Wireless T/ apparatus	JH
"	29.8.17		Attended a lecture on the effects of the new mustard gas used by the Germans	JH

Army Form C. 2118.

WAR DIARY
or
INTELLIGENCE SUMMARY
(Erase heading not required.)

Instructions regarding War Diaries and Intelligence Summaries are contained in F. S. Regs., Part II. and the Staff Manual respectively. Title Pages will be prepared in manuscript.

Place	Date	Hour	Summary of Events and Information	Remarks and references to Appendices
ST EREN	30.8.17		Went futher on in this area examining + classifying. Bad weather for some days now + little sunshine	
"	31.8.17	10.55	MO to Pauley AOC H.T. arrived from there for duty with this Unit	

Forms: Sialcote Cav: F'd Amb
46 Cav: Divn:

J.J. Irwin
Major I.M.S.

Medical

Serial No. 240.

COMMITTEE FOR THE
MEDICAL HISTORY OF THE WAR
Date 12 DEC. 1917

Original

R/R. 1917

Confidential

War Diary
of
Anzac Mounted Division

From 1.9.17.   to 30.9.17.

(Vol. XXXII)

Army Form C. 2118.

Original

medical

WAR DIARY
OR
INTELLIGENCE SUMMARY

(Erase heading not required.)

Vol XXXII

Instructions regarding War Diaries and Intelligence ... are contained in F. S. Regs., Part II. ... Staff Manual respectively. Title Pages will be prepared in manuscript.

Place	Date	Hour	Summary of Events and Information	Remarks and references to Appendices
ST. CREN	1.9.17		War Diary VXXXI forwarded to A.D.M.S. Received A.D.M.S. No 19/4050 re "Compilation of B 213."	
"	2.9.17		Cash statement and regimental rolls sent to Cont of Military Accounts	
"	3.9.17		Capt-Lieut R.A.M.C. reported from detached duty with No 102 Field Ambulance	
"	4.9.17		Capt-Hawkins took over temporary command of Jodhpur C.F.A. in addition to his own duties. All officers on the strength were inspected by the D.R. this evening. Received all additional Hospital Orders.	
	5.9.17		—	
	6.9.17		—	
	7.9.17		Three Riding Horses - R2- received from the base.	

Army Form C. 2118.

WAR DIARY
or
INTELLIGENCE SUMMARY
(Erase heading not required.)

Instructions regarding War Diaries and Intelligence
Summaries are contained in F. S. Regs., Part II.
and the Staff Manual respectively. Title Pages
will be prepared in manuscript.

Place	Date	Hour	Summary of Events and Information	Remarks and references to Appendices
ST CREPY	8.9.17		Medical Officers attended a class at Eubourn O.F.A. in Lillers m) Field Medical Card	
	9.9.17		Box Respirators drill carried out twice weekly at present all men have worn the Respirator for one hour continuously	
	10.9.17		—	
	11.9.17		Revd McCann joined the Unit 15-day Reserve AWMS No M/4180	
	12.9.17		Revd Kalapurachala IMS to be transferred for duty in 1st Corps No M/4197 3rd Lancers	
	13.9.17		Capt. Renow RAMC proceeded on leave to U.K. Received AWMS No M/4197	
	14.9.17			
	15.9.17		No 2017 Naich KENSHI AB Corps has been awarded for Indian Meritorious Service Medal Received AWMS No M/4220 re Restoration of Devastated Areas	

Army Form C. 2118.

WAR DIARY
or
INTELLIGENCE SUMMARY

(Erase heading not required.)

Place	Date	Hour	Summary of Events and Information	Remarks and references to Appendices
ST CREN	16.9.17			
	17.9.17		No 7727 I/Sht VALLAYAT A.H. Corps transferred for duty with Lucknow CFA. Capt Cory RAMC re-joined for duty with the Unit	
	18.9.17		Men standing for inoculation commenced Inoculation last 2-3 days	
	19.9.17		Two L.C.S. Wagons detailed for duty with No 1 Sect at ATHIES. Received A&MMS No 19/428.	
	20.9.17			
	21.9.17		Received A&MMS No 114/816 re "Treatment of Symptoms of" for chln. ethyl. sulphide	
	22.9.17		Party of H.IS Corps men sent to Div H.Qrs for fatigue duty - preparing Camp	
	23.9.17		Received A&MMS No 1320 re Instruments returned and No 1544 re Tooth Brushes for the Lines	

Army Form C. 2118.

WAR DIARY
or
INTELLIGENCE SUMMARY
(Erase heading not required.)

Place	Date	Hour	Summary of Events and Information	Remarks and references to Appendices
ST OMER	24.9.17		Received AFMS No 74/435 qu "Carriage of M.T. Stretcher Carriers"	
"	25.9.17		On Riding Horse and one L.D Mule evacuated to MVS Third Army R.O No 1113 re "Shortage of Information" brought to the notice of all personnel.	
"	26.9.17		Received AQMG's No 438 re "So-Called" and No 457 re "Watch Ends" Lieut-Colonel 145172 joined the Unit for duty	
"	27.9.17		Received AFMS No 74/615 re "Medical Equipment"	
"	28.9.17		Sergt Morris ASC joined for duty on Supply Supp. with the Unit.	
"	29.9.17		Div R.O. re Trotting of L.D. Mules re on the harness, now issued, read out on parade	
"	30.9.17		— — —	

Comm²: Sialcote Cav: F'd Amb:
1/1 Cav: Div²:

(Original)
(OR 107)

Memories
240

Confidential

War Diary

of

31st 1st Cavalry Field Ambulance

From 1.10.17.   To 31.10.17.

Vol. XXXIII

COMMITTEE FOR THE
MEDICAL HISTORY OF THE WAR
Date 8 FEB. 1918

Original

Army Form C. 2118

Melicut

WAR DIARY
or
INTELLIGENCE SUMMARY. VOL XXXII

(Erase heading not required.)

Instructions regarding War Diaries and Intelligence Summaries are contained in F. S. Regs., Part II. and the Staff Manual respectively. Title pages will be prepared in manuscript.

Place	Date	Hour	Summary of Events and Information	Remarks and references to Appendices
ST CREN	1.10.17		During the last month the Sunbeam Ambulance Car has been fitted with heating apparatus inside the car - a great improvement as these cars are sometimes very cold in winter. No car available as yet - huts very much in need of lining	JM
"	2.10.17		War Diary Vol XXXII forwarded to ADMS Deputation titles and Indent Account for Sept. sent to 7 Corp. Wkly Rets	JM
"	3.10.17		Received two 110 gal tanks for storage of drinking water - now nearly sufficient	JM
"	4.10.17		Received B.A.M.S. (No. 14460 re Cars not being returned to Medical Units of the Division beyond 14 days. Letter from D.H. 111th Army re "Gang of Thieves" received & communicated to all concerned	JM
"	5.10.17		Capt=Quin R.A.M.C reported his departure 15 days duty with the 2nd Cavalry Division.	JM
"	6.10.17		ADMS and OC Field Squadron visited the Unit to settle the greater of huts for the winter	JM

J Moore
Major RAMC

Army Form C. 2118

WAR DIARY
or
INTELLIGENCE SUMMARY.
(Erase heading not required.)

Instructions regarding War Diaries and Intelligence Summaries are contained in F. S. Regs., Part II. and the Staff Manual respectively. Title pages will be prepared in manuscript.

Place	Date	Hour	Summary of Events and Information	Remarks and references to Appendices
ST CREN	7.10.17		Winter time came into use this morning. Frost during the night. Heavy rain & wind later.	JH
"	8.10.17		Received ADMS No M/4588	JH
"	9.10.17		Received one copy each 1 Cav. Corps code names and Cavalry Corps Station Code calls. Received ADMS No M/4615 + M/4602	JH
	10.10.17		- - -	
	11.10.17		Very bad weather again, mostly the hay (clover) cut and stacked by the Unit will be spoilt, was except for falling	JH
"	12.10.17		In ADMS notifies that sanction has been obtained to add to Echelon 1 Water Cart + 1 Cooks Cart. The water cart in carrying necessary and the cooks cart well allow of easier work which is important in cross country work.	JH
"	13.10.17		No 052/6911 Serj: Fawden reported from base. No dispatches to establishment. Received ADMS No M/4670. No Lk 085 Stephenson Table Box attached S.O. Dix Tps. was thought to have died yesterday evening at 6 p.m. all articles & papers received from the body	JH

T2134. Wt. W708—776. 500000. 4/15. Sir J. C. & S.

Army Form C.2118

WAR DIARY
or
INTELLIGENCE SUMMARY.
(Erase heading not required.)

Instructions regarding War Diaries and Intelligence
Summaries are contained in F. S. Regs., Part II.
and the Staff Manual respectively. Title pages
will be prepared in manuscript.

Place	Date	Hour	Summary of Events and Information	Remarks and references to Appendices
ST CREN	14.10.17		Oost-Winter on N° 865 Ar/31 Bux. Cause of death - Heart failure in early stays. Pneumonia. Valuables & articles belonging to above sent to S.O. Div Troops	JU
"	15.10.17		One Bearer A/S Corps arrived for duty at Lucknow C.F.S	JU
"	16.10.17		Intynrelu Cresson left the Unit to-day on transfer to the 3rd Cavalry Division. Reyt-Fawcor transferred to take details Lucknow Cav. Brigade	JU
"	17.10.17		Received A/SM/S N° M/4716. Submitted on the 16th a return to the A/S.M/S re necessary repairs to hospital Buildings	JU
"	18.10.17		Received A/SM/S N° M/4718	JU
"	19.10.17		Tactical Field Ambulance exercise by Lucknow C.F.A Received A/SM/S N° M/4731	JU
"	20.10.17		—	
"	21.10.17		Received A/SM/S N° M/4759 re "Clothing infected with lice" Received 3rd Army R.O.1183 re "Fires now put on parade"	JU

Army Form C.2118

WAR DIARY
or
INTELLIGENCE SUMMARY.
(Erase heading not required.)

Instructions regarding War Diaries and Intelligence Summaries are contained in F. S. Regs., Part II. and the Staff Manual respectively. Title pages will be prepared in manuscript.

Place	Date	Hour	Summary of Events and Information	Remarks and references to Appendices
STCREM	22.10.17		Received Circular N° SS. 393 Censorship Orders & Replenishing - circulated	JM
"	23.10.17		—	
"	24.10.17		Two A.V.S. Corps men reported from duty at the Base	JM
"	25.10.17		Failed review by Ambala C.F.A. Two Units provided 11 A.V.S. Corps men as stretcher bearers. Two officers attended. Received A.S.M.S N° M/4818.	JM
"	26.10.17		Received A.S.M.S N°M/4825 & M/4848. 8SMS Cavalry Corps visited the Unit - in connection with messing accommodation	JM
"	27.10.17		—	
"	28.10.17		Received Army Council Instruction N°1754 of 10/6.	JM
"	29.10.17		Bath house completed; no other work taken in hand by F-Squadron	
"	30.10.17		—	
"	31.10.17		Fine almost warm weather. Received A.S.M.S N°14/4921 re Tetanus.	JM

Comm: Sialcote Cav: F⁴ Amb
1/6 Cav: Division

J M Munro
Major I.M.S.

Measles

240

Confidential

War Diary

of

SIALKOT Cavalry Field Ambulance

From 1.11.17 to 30.11.17

(Vol XXXIV)

COMMITTEE FOR THE
MEDICAL HISTORY OF THE WAR
Date -8 FEB. 1918

Army Form C. 2118.

WAR DIARY
or
~~INTELLIGENCE SUMMARY.~~   Vol. XXXIV
(Erase heading not required.)

Instructions regarding War Diaries and Intelligence Summaries are contained in F. S. Regs., Part II. and the Staff Manual respectively. Title pages will be prepared in manuscript.

Place	Date	Hour	Summary of Events and Information	Remarks and references to Appendices
ST. OREN	1.11.17		Commenced to-day a series of lectures on Organisation of the Medical Services. Circular re: to Officers of the Unit and M.Os. of Units in the neighbourhood.	
"	2.11.17		War Diary Vol XXXIII forwarded to A.D.M.S. Attended a Court of Inquiry at No 5. C.C.S. to investigate a case of injury by a French soldier evacuated by this Unit. Received A.D.M.S. No M/4925	
"	3.11.17		No M/8113 Corpl 147477 M.I.R. joined from base for duty with the Unit. Acquittance Rolls and Cash Account for October sent to Compt. Milt. Acct.	
"	4.11.17		No 61242 Pte Dawson. R.A.M.C. joined from Army Vet. Park for duty with the Unit.	
"	5.11.17		— — — — — —	
"	6.11.17		Nissen huts for the Unit arrived on the 1st but no more 15 put them up on yet.	

Army Form C. 2118.

WAR DIARY
or
INTELLIGENCE SUMMARY.
(Erase heading not required.)

Instructions regarding War Diaries and Intelligence Summaries are contained in F. S. Regs., Part II. and the Staff Manual respectively. Title pages will be prepared in manuscript.

Place	Date	Hour	Summary of Events and Information	Remarks and references to Appendices
ST CREN	7.11.17		Received A.O.M.S. No M/5007 re Surgical Operations in the front area	JH
"	8.11.17		— — — — — — — — — —	
"	9.11.17		No 26052 Cpl FARRELL R.A.M.C. joined for duty on transfer with the Unit. No 74/035706 Drover STEVENS proceeded to V.22 Vet. School for course of cold shoeing	JH
"	10.11.17		Received NO.S.S.193. Standing Orders for Defence against Gas	JH
"	11.11.17		11 A.S.Corps men of this Unit are away daily on fatigues reported to AQMG that these men were much needed here for erection of hospital huts.	JH
"	12.11.17		Woolwich fatigues from to-day. Received Special Order	JH
"	13.11.17		Drivers Crawley, Cooke + Hambling transferred to No 4 Cavalry Brown Reserve Park	JH

WAR DIARY
or
INTELLIGENCE SUMMARY.
(Erase heading not required.)

Army Form C. 2118.

Place	Date	Hour	Summary of Events and Information	Remarks and references to Appendices
ST CREN	13.11.17		Three HT Drivers joined for duty with the Unit 3 from Reserve Park and 2 from 4 H.T. Coy.	JH
"	14.11.17		Received ADMS No M/5003 re the of time expired Men and Noncoms, and No M/5010 re Use of "B.I.P."	JH
"	15.11.17		Published addendum to Standing Orders 9th Mtd division how personnel of 1st and 1/5 Echelon is carried. Attended a conference as representative of ADMS 9 at 11 AM S Officer Cav. Corps H.Q.	JH
"	16.11.17		Received ADMS No M/5026 re "Ready & Precautionary zones" regarding Gas Defence.	JH
"	17.11.17		Notified Rattak Brigade change in command of Tech Mounted Division unit in event of Unit being ready for operation.	JH

Army Form C. 2118.

WAR DIARY
or
INTELLIGENCE SUMMARY.
(Erase heading not required.)

Place	Date	Hour	Summary of Events and Information	Remarks and references to Appendices
YTCREN	18.11.17		Requested A.D.M.S to arrange for representative from VII Corps to take over Rest Station Equipment. Received A.D.M.S No. M/5074 and M/5075	
"	19.11.17		Received information that the Cavalry Corps will probably take part in active operations at an early date. Preparations made accordingly. All patients convalescent from Rest station Corp FARRELL sent to Walking Wounded Collecting Station at TINCOURT for the purpose of receiving casualties of Cavalry Corps coming through the station.	
"	20.11.17		One Motor Ambulance proceeded for duty at A.D.M.S. Hqrs. 5 Echelon of Personnel left. Yesterday the Unit yesterday. Transport moved 2 hours after to move.	
FINS	21.11.17		Received orders to move at 2.10 a.m. very dark + raining. Unit + 18 Section Excharers of F.A. moved out at 4 a.m. Considerable delay in getting away from starting point. Column moved off to CENTRAL TOWN FARM afterwards	

Army Form C. 2118.

WAR DIARY
or
INTELLIGENCE SUMMARY.
(Erase heading not required.)

Instructions regarding War Diaries and Intelligence Summaries are contained in F.S. Regs., Part II. and the Staff Manual respectively. Title pages will be prepared in manuscript.

Place	Date	Hour	Summary of Events and Information	Remarks and references to Appendices
FINS	21.11.17		Marched via PERRONNE to a camping ground west of FINS. Roads heavy, rain part of the way; company found beds in huts. The Unit was attached to Australs Brigade on going into huts for SAA to go - which we had about 1½ miles away. Rack Mounted Sections reported strength + a.o. Duet for riding horses at BArtHom came of sudden colics. Send own vets. Finds shelters. Nearly pain by Infantry but was endeavoring of Division veterinary mf. Am riding horse evacuated to Mobile Vet section	JH
"	22.11.17		Windy & cloudy. No orders for Division moving yet. Our C.O.'s movement order to Hucknow E.C.B. information received at night that the Division would move tomorrow to St Christ again tomorrow	JH
ST CHRIST	23.11.17		The Unit moved to ST CHRIST to-day and took over huts as previously occupied by Lucknow Sta. March commenced at 12 noon. Arrived at 4.15. Received intimation that tomorrow the Unit would be on one hours notice to move	JH
"	24.11.17		Attention of all concerned drawn to Defence March Discipline	

Army Form C. 2118.

WAR DIARY
or
INTELLIGENCE SUMMARY.
(Erase heading not required.)

Instructions regarding War Diaries and Intelligence Summaries are contained in F. S. Regs., Part II. and the Staff Manual respectively. Title pages will be prepared in manuscript.

Place	Date	Hour	Summary of Events and Information	Remarks and references to Appendices
ST CHRIST	24.11.17		Accommodation fair but poor; Sore of huts not yet completed and no stoves. Intimation received at night that the Division will move at about 6 a.m.	JH
"	25.11.17		The Unit marched to VILLERS FAUCON 8-day train at 6 a.m. On march - my self + Corporal went, arrived at 11.30 am Park Member + Driver O.C. Report to Rabbit Isle 4 do as requested by A.D.M.S. Information received that Division will move back again at once. Left at 3.30 pm Division got more back again on the way. Just returned VILLERS FAUCON	JH
"	26.11.17		S.R.O. No. 2855 communicated to all personnel of the Unit	JH
"	27.11.17		Army Service H.T. transferred for duty with fishleer C.T.C. Received A.O.M.S. No. M/56/27	JH
"	28.11.17		Ward Orderly Abdul Wahed reported from detached duty	JH
"	29.11.17		Intimation received that the Division will take over part of the line to-morrow in the neighbourhood of TEMPLEUX + ROISEL. Proceeded to these places to see A.D.S. in the afternoon. Arrangements were made. Main part of the Unit goes to BEAULIT	JH

Army Form C. 2118.

WAR DIARY
or
INTELLIGENCE SUMMARY.
(Erase heading not required.)

Instructions regarding War Diaries and Intelligence Summaries are contained in F. S. Regs., Part II. and the Staff Manual respectively. Title pages will be prepared in manuscript.

Place	Date	Hour	Summary of Events and Information	Remarks and references to Appendices
ST CHRIST	29/11/17		A.D.S put to JEAN COURT. Erected others regularly manned & accordingly	
"	30.11.17		One Horse Ambulance received from Railhead. Proceeded to JEAN COURT to await instruction of unit to return relieve team to line cancelled. Had to get ready to move to another area as soon as possible. Marched out at 14.40 in whole unit except guard of 4 men. Received orders on the way. Proceeded to VILLERS FAUCON. Arrived there at 18 pm. Part rooms & parents in finding harness.	

Comd: **Sialcote Cav: Fd Amb**
d/r **Cav: Divis:**

Original
Medical

(240)

Confidential.

War Diary

of

3rd Cat Lac Fld Ambulance

(Vol XXXV)

From 1.12.17

Original

Army Form C. 2118.
Medical

WAR DIARY
or
INTELLIGENCE SUMMARY
(Erase heading not required.)

Vol. XXXV

Place	Date	Hour	Summary of Events and Information	Remarks and references to Appendices
VILLERS FAUCON	1.12.17		Received orders last night that O.C. Ambulance and each Umentil Section will report to Drakali Brigade H.Q. at dawn. Left bivouac at 5 a.m. and proceeded to Bde H.Q. In the meantime had orders to move to position of readiness near PEIZIERES and were moving when the P.M. Section joined up. Proceeded in rear of the Brigade to a position between EPEHY and ST. EMELIE at about 9 a.m. The Brigade was ordered to move to position N.W. of PEIZIERE - this having been ordered to proceed to its objective. 15th Brigade remained in this position throughout the day. At about 12.30 p.m. part of the area was shelled by the enemy; there were 7 casualties - 1 severe. These were attended to by M.O. Units assisted by Officer of the Ambulance and were collected near the road. The cases were eventually evacuated by Horse Ambulances. At 2 p.m. 4 Motor Ambulance cars were ordered up to HEDICOURT. They arrived about 5 p.m. coming via EPEHY. At 4.15 p.m. heavy shelling by the enemy over the whole area. Only two casualties - 1 officer. Both horses killed. Two cases evacuated by Horse Ambulance. Informed an Officer of F.UDICOURT.	

Cont. Stables Group - A.M.S.

Army Form C. 2118.

WAR DIARY
or
INTELLIGENCE SUMMARY
(Erase heading not required.)

Instructions regarding War Diaries and Intelligence Summaries are contained in F. S. Regs, Part II. and the Staff Manual respectively. Title pages will be prepared in manuscript.

Place	Date	Hour	Summary of Events and Information	Remarks and references to Appendices
VILLERS FAUCON	1.12.17		Information received that the Brigade would send in a dismounted party. Parts of A.K.Coy men sent up to HEUDICOURT in relief of Ambulance Bans	
"	2.12.17		Sent up 2 Horse Ambulances, 1 Medical Officer and 4 Bearers to HEUDICOURT at 8.45 am. with instructions to proceed to Regt. Aid Post beyond HEUDICOURT. Proceeded to HEUDICOURT with 2 Motor Ambulances and 8 bearers: arranged for accommodation of bearers and for the work at Reg. Aid Post - kept very busy in 1 November and that evacuation. Sent up 2 more Motor Ambulances + 1 Horse Ambulance with 1 Medical Officer + 4 Bearers. The bearers - Ambulances evacuated 28 wounded during the night. Received orders about 11.30 p.m. that the Division would move back to other area to morrow. D.A.D. Rafiuddin Khan and 10 men reported from TEMPLEUX. 1 wounded evacuated from TEMPLEUX by the 10 U.Ambulance 3rd Ward Orderly Rajaram Singh rejoined from detached duty	

Army Form C. 2118.

WAR DIARY
or
INTELLIGENCE SUMMARY.
(Erase heading not required.)

Instructions regarding War Diaries and Intelligence Summaries are contained in F. S. Regs., Part II. and the Staff Manual respectively. Title pages will be prepared in manuscript.

Place	Date	Hour	Summary of Events and Information	Remarks and references to Appendices
ST CHRIST	3.12.17		The Unit moved north to ST CHRIST to-day, leaving at 4.45 am arriving at 2.35 pm. Received from HEUDICOURT Camp on by Motor and Horse Ambulances. Dismounted men marched all the way.	JW
"	4.12.17		No 2/2535 A/Cpl FREELOVE J. A/Cpl H.T. joined for duty vice No 88617 A/Cpl (Crist of Enquiry) the Unit. Received No 88617.	JW
"	5.12.17		Received O.C.M.S. No M/5268	
"	6.12.17		8 Cavalry Pattern Stretchers received War Diary Vol XXIX forwarded to A.D.M.S. Cash accounts for November sent to Field Cashier. Med. Hist. Capt FARRELL R.A.M.C returned from duty at No 5 C.C.S	JW
"	7.12.17		Maps and Notes returned to A.D.M.S. Received No B.M. 530 Reubrick "Use in event of Light and fires in this area: read out on parade. Fairly hard frost last 2 - 3 days.	JW

Army Form C. 2118.

WAR DIARY
or
INTELLIGENCE SUMMARY.

(Erase heading not required.)

Instructions regarding War Diaries and Intelligence Summaries are contained in F.S. Regs., Part II. and the Staff Manual respectively. Title pages will be prepared in manuscript.

Place	Date	Hour	Summary of Events and Information	Remarks and references to Appendices
S? CHR2 187	8-12-17		Third Army Routine Orders No 1326 & 1327 brought to the notice of all concerned. Knew this morning and rainfall continued in the evening that the Krew Bohemean Division.	JW
	9.12.17		Driver WILSON F.C. transferred for duty with Divisional C.F.T. Lieut Chaudhri 148 detailed as M.T. Officer to 2nd Cavalry Infantry Battalion.	JW
	10.12.17		Regimental Field Squadron Supply baths & fire worn out work exempted completed but they are received. Received orders No M/557? in good of White towels communicated to all of concerned.	JW
	11.12.17		—	
	12.12.17		Marching Orders received 8-day which Unit marched out and received article of equipment necessary Lieut Chaudhri proceeded as M.T.O. 2nd Cavalry Infantry Battalion.	JW

A 5834 Wt. W4973/M687 750,000 8/16 D.D. & L. Ltd. Forms/C.2118/13

Army Form C. 2118.

WAR DIARY
or
INTELLIGENCE SUMMARY.
(Erase heading not required.)

Instructions regarding War Diaries and Intelligence Summaries are contained in F.S. Regs., Part II. and the Staff Manual respectively. Title pages will be prepared in manuscript.

Place	Date	Hour	Summary of Events and Information	Remarks and references to Appendices
S.CHRIST	13.12.17		Capt Hurst, 1 batman and 2 Ward Orderlies and cook proceeded for temporary duty at Lusburn C.C.Station	JW
"	14.12.17		One L.D. Horse evacuated to Milkil Vet. Sectn. Received ADMS No M/5263. 5162 + 5217	JW
"	15.12.17		All authorised preventive measures against Trench Feet. Received ADMS No M/5657	JW
"	16.12.17		Received SS615 "Cohesion in the Field" other ADMS No 5282. Rain for past few days	JW
"	17.12.17		Received ADMS No 55512 + 5514. Heavy fall of snow during the night - 8-10 inches	JW
"	18.12.17		In spite of early morning huts still covered carried out on material has not yet been received. Received ADMS No 55110 + 5541. Very hard frost and high wind during the night. Many loads docked from dug-outs, snow and can't build until conditions. Brigade moved	JW

Army Form C. 2118.

WAR DIARY
or
INTELLIGENCE SUMMARY.

(Erase heading not required.)

Instructions regarding War Diaries and Intelligence Summaries are contained in F.S. Regs., Part II. and the Staff Manual respectively. Title pages will be prepared in manuscript.

Place	Date	Hour	Summary of Events and Information	Remarks and references to Appendices
ST CHRIST	19.12.17		Received A.C.M.S. No 3857/2 & No 5557/1. Attention Jack Reserve Officer drawn to these	JW
	20.12.17		—	
	21.12.17		The Cavalry Corps is to surrender the Fifth Army Routine Orders received	JW
	22.12.17		Received A.C.M.S. No 5593 & 5594	JW
	23.12.17		All rum rations inspected at length - pouch cases turned in at Supt Sanitary 10 ASC men inoculated	JW
			to ROISEL for Fatigue duty	
	24.12.17		Attention of all Officers drawn to the extreme importance of all records of enemy in all stores, clothing &c Private Stevens returned from course of extra driving	JW
	25.12.17		Snow during the night but heavy again in afternoon. Snow Column in Sreator at 6 pm but eventually cancelled. No British personnel held dep. but two severely wounded	JW

O.H.M.S. Corporal
A 583+ Wt. W 4973/M687 750,000 8/16 D.D. & L. Ltd. Forms/C.2118/13.

Army Form C. 2118.

WAR DIARY
or
INTELLIGENCE SUMMARY.
(Erase heading not required.)

Instructions regarding War Diaries and Intelligence Summaries are contained in F.S. Regs., Part II. and the Staff Manual respectively. Title pages will be prepared in manuscript.

Place	Date	Hour	Summary of Events and Information	Remarks and references to Appendices
SICHRIST	26.12.17		Intimation received that no Bryah of the Division is now under 1 hour notice. Received A.F.W.S. No 5770 & 5718	
"	27.12.17		Mr Wilton sent on to Advance Workshop for materials and examination in local repair. 1st Pittock reported from Company duty at Ambala CAA. Received AFWS No 5735 & 5742 re "Self-inflicted Wounds."	
"	28.12.17		Received AFWS No 5746 re Return of members of French Red Cross Nurr. Front in Prior camps.	
"	29.12.17		Received AFWS No 5742 re "Irelund-Poshies cases."	
"	30.12.17		1 British O.R. and 4 Indians 1 Motor Ambulance and Water Cart proceeded for duty not working party at Sikhe country	
"	31.12.17		Capt Hurst M.O. R.S. U.S.A. transferred for duty with Lucknow C. C. station	

Comdt: Sialcote Cav: F^d Amb
6th Cav: Divisⁿ

Original

Confidential

(240)

well cut

Ymca.

War Diary
of
SIALKOT CAV. FIELD AMBULANCE.

No. 1. 1. 76

COMMITTEE FOR THE
MEDICAL HISTORY OF THE WAR
Date 12 JUL 1919

Vol. XXXVI

Original

Medical

Army Form C. 2118.

WAR DIARY
or
INTELLIGENCE SUMMARY.
(Erase heading not required.)

Vol XXXVI

Instructions regarding War Diaries and Intelligence Summaries are contained in F.S. Regs., Part II. and the Staff Manual respectively. Title pages will be prepared in manuscript.

Place	Date	Hour	Summary of Events and Information	Remarks and references to Appendices
ST CHRIST	1.1.18		Received ADMS No 3. attention of all Medical Officers drawn to the circular	JW
	2.1.18		Cash statements & accounts for Dec. 17 sent to Field Comb Military Accounts. Received ADMS No 12 re Felling 1) Medical Cards. Party proceeded with forward area for duty with a working party.	JW
	3.1.18		—	—
	4.1.18		Reference B.R.O. re Economy in Manpower and Material. Some suggestions sent to ADMS to-day. Received ADMS P.N.12/1. 86 & 87	JW
	5.1.18		Rev Capt Wymer R.C. joined for duty with the Unit. Received ADMS No 110 - attention of all Medical Officers drawn to this	JW
	6.1.18		Received No A1579 from D.D.S+T re Army re Precautions be taken for prevention of damage by frost to M.T. Vehicles. Read out to all M.T. personnel. Received ADMS No 15 re Felling in) Medical Cards	JW

Army Form C. 2118.

WAR DIARY
or
INTELLIGENCE SUMMARY.
(Erase heading not required.)

Instructions regarding War Diaries and Intelligence Summaries are contained in F.S. Regs., Part II. and the Staff Manual respectively. Title pages will be prepared in manuscript.

Place	Date	Hour	Summary of Events and Information	Remarks and references to Appendices
ST CHRIST	7.1.18		Intimation received that any location must always be given on reporting infectious cases	AH
	8.1.18		A party from the Unit proceeded for duty with a Mtn Btty in the forward area. 1 Officer Hospital Orderlies Rct Chand proceeded the Indian Distn pushed Service Medal	AH
	9.1.18		Orders issued re Water filling point	AH
	10.1.18		OC & D Horse evacuated sick. Mr Mrs Powis reported for duty from Ambala C.F.H. Shaw return	AH
	11.1.18		Received A.C.M.S. N° 271 & 272	AH
	12.1.18		Shaw Scheme came into operation from midnight 11/12. With Building work as probable against Frozen operation commenced	AH
	13.1.18		Received A.C.M.S. N° 336 & 335	AH
	14.1.18		Attended a lecture given by Colonel Simpson to 1st Army. Visited N° 1 Working Party at HERVILLY	AH

A 5834 Wt. W 4973/M687 750,000 8/16 D.D. & L. Ltd. Forms/C.2118/13

Army Form C. 2118.

WAR DIARY
or
INTELLIGENCE SUMMARY.
(Erase heading not required.)

Instructions regarding War Diaries and Intelligence Summaries are contained in F. S. Regs., Part II. and the Staff Manual respectively. Title pages will be prepared in manuscript.

Place	Date	Hour	Summary of Events and Information	Remarks and references to Appendices
ST CHRIST	15.1.18		Their scheme came again into operation at 6 pm after five weeks first thaw set in yesterday; rain during the day	All
"	16.1.18		One L.D. Mule arrived from railhead. Bearer No 32,27 Numbers evacuated to Lucknow C.C.D arrived off the chinjest	All
"	17.1.18		Received arms No 125 & 280	All
"	18.1.18		Fresh iron rations issued today and all old cloth covering. Received arms Nos 1,138 & 489.	All
"	19.1.18		Received arms No. 464 & 465	All
"	20.1.18		One Bearer A.B.Corps and one Cook Bt Corps arrived for the Base for duty with the Unit.	All
"	21.1.18		Their restrictions ceased at 6 p.m. Received WOWS No 531 Returned to Supel Major Ashrek Ida Cole Horse and Station Cold Callo of Units of L Cavalry Division	All
	22.1.18			
	23.1.18		All R.a.m.c personnel examined for Category. All A Category	All

A 3834 Wt. W 4973/M687 750,000 8/16 D. D. & L. Ltd. Forms/C.2118/13.

Army Form C. 2118.

WAR DIARY
or
INTELLIGENCE SUMMARY.
(Erase heading not required.)

Place	Date	Hour	Summary of Events and Information	Remarks and references to Appendices
ST CHRIST	24.1.18		Intimation received that Coy proceeded for Mt.s Whitwell shortly to proceed to A.D.S and M.D.S in area occupied by the 24th Division. The Division in turn now accepts the line. B.R.O N.D 1872 re Wool paper substitution on Order book. Copies of F.R.O N.D 1871 + 1941 re damage to Lipto circulated and posted in Order board	M
"	25.1.18		Orr Stocks transferred to Lucknow C.C.S for temporary duty there. Visited Berner + Templeux to arrange for accommodation there to proceeded to hard places	M
"	26.1.18		Lieut Chardin proceeded for duty with N°4 Workers Party. Received A.C.S.M.S N° 609 + 628	M
"	27.1.18		Capt Hawkins + party proceeded for duty at A.D.S at TEMPLEUX and M.D.S at BERNES. Received A.C.S.M.S N° 677 + 679.	M
"	28.1.18		Proceeded to Templeux. Received A.C.S.M.S N° 709 + 715	M

Army Form C. 2118.

WAR DIARY
or
INTELLIGENCE SUMMARY.
(Erase heading not required.)

Instructions regarding War Diaries and Intelligence Summaries are contained in F. S. Regs., Part II. and the Staff Manual respectively. Title pages will be prepared in manuscript.

Place	Date	Hour	Summary of Events and Information	Remarks and references to Appendices
ST CHRIST	29/1/18		All for Dushmatis inspected by Brigade Sgt N.C.O. all containers changed	
	30/1/18		Received A.O.Nos No 766	
	31/1/18		The Sergt Major proceeded to-day to new area in the neighbourhood of Amiens. Received A.O.Nos No 785 + 786	

Comdg: Siacote Cav. 1m Amb
1st Cav: Divisn:

Medical

240

COMMITTEE FOR THE
MEDICAL HISTORY OF THE WAR
Date 12 JUL 1918

Confidential

War Diary
of
2nd Cav. Field Ambulance

from 1.1.18. to 28.2.18

(Vol XXXVII)

original

2/7/18

Army Form C. 2118.

Medical

original

WAR DIARY
or
INTELLIGENCE SUMMARY.
(Erase heading not required.)

Vol. XXXVII

Instructions regarding War Diaries and Intelligence
Summaries are contained in F. S. Regs., Part II.
and the Staff Manual respectively. Title pages
will be prepared in manuscript.

Place	Date	Hour	Summary of Events and Information	Remarks and references to Appendices
Field	1/2/18		Col. Statement & acquittance rolls & quarterly payment to F&M Entitled WIBST accounts. I.F.F.P. Advance pay of 1.30 & 30 B.D.P. on 1st from No. 2 C.F.A. All ranks warned not to expect pay. 2 dogs put at 6 dock free. On return No. 9 Off B.O.C. return from the train. W.H	
	2/2/18		No 2.9/18.B Coste Sgt. Belcher Sgt Sr & Cpl. arrived ½ day Est He sent. W.H	
	3/2/18		Party driving duty at the A.D.S. Lieut Templeton one officer & escorts party from the unit but knows when & Bde & the area & arrives. Per Diary Vol XXXVI forwarded to A.D.M.S. Party of 15 Indians detached for duty at Bde Dump. W.H	
	4/2/18		Unit marched ½ day at 10 a.m. & arrived at HARBONNIERES at 3.30 p.m. Most of Indian personnel was forward by train a/c to 5th. Billets & men & camels sent forward. G.M	
	5/2/18		Unit marched ½ day at 8 a.m. through & RUMIGNY arrived at 3.30 p.m. Indian personnel marched from AMIENS station Unit. March of about 28 kilometres day in spite bad roads. W.H	

WAR DIARY
or
INTELLIGENCE SUMMARY.

(Erase heading not required.)

Army Form C. 2118.

Place	Date	Hour	Summary of Events and Information	Remarks and references to Appendices
Field	5/2/18		Capt H.P. HAWKINS R.A.M.C. & 2 H.T. Drivers proceeded on leave to U.K. Received No. SS. 5235 A Rogalatter to railway siding. W.P.H.	
	7/2/18		Pte. No. 28633 Pte EVERLEY R.A.M.C. Transferred to 4th Can. Div. H.Q. W.P.H.	
	8/2/18		4th Can Div. Nothing to Report. W.P.H.	
	9/2/18		Col. Harris KING W. Transferred to H.R. 33rd Div. W.P.H.	
	10/2/18		Lt.-Col. URWIN J.J. Gh.S. proceeded on leave to U.K. Temporary command of the unit taken over by Capt R.M. LONG R.A.M.C. of Mobile C.F.D. Issuer. Dr. ROBBINS A.S.C.H.T. reported his arrival on duty on return from Col. who had gone to a Course to hold from 11-2-18. See note. A.S.C. R.O.S/104 SS/D/136 dt 2-2-18.	
	11/2/18		A.D.M.S. inspected hospital. Copying of Orders started in accordance with orders received from A.D.M.S. W.P.H.	
	12/2/18		Nothing to Note W.P.H.	
	13/2/18		Mallein test applied to all animals of the unit W.P.H.	
	14/2/18		Lt. THEROW R. Reeve reported his arrival of duty on return from leave W.P.H.	

Army Form C. 2118.

WAR DIARY
or
INTELLIGENCE SUMMARY.
(Erase heading not required.)

Instructions regarding War Diaries and Intelligence Summaries are contained in F. S. Regs., Part II. and the Staff Manual respectively. Title pages will be prepared in manuscript.

Place	Date	Hour	Summary of Events and Information	Remarks and references to Appendices
Field	15/7/18		Party from the unit doing duty at A.D.S. TEMPLEUX returned. Lt. CHAUDHRI. 1 N.C.O. & party doing duty with the working party at HERVILLY returned. W/M	
	16/7/18		Recall of Mallein tests reported to be all negative. W/M	
	17/7/18		Capt. PERRY. D. Rawn. 17th Can. Inf.Bn. temporarily commanded of the unit from Capt LANG. W/M	
	18/7/18		ARO No. 3397 S. boo of M.Sh. Sergts. Sereeed & Commemorated & all contesty. W/M	
	19/7/18		Dr DUCKWORTH No. T/96651. R.S.C H.T. reported the unit having been discharged to duty from No 4 C.F.D. M/T/23366 Corpl. MAM Div S.B.T. ceases having been evacuated from No 4 C.F.D. 1 Week R.S. a death off the strength. W/M	
	20/7/18		No. 3080. Pte HORTON Yorks Hussars Rgt having been evacuated by No 1. C.F.D. & H. Sicknesy Hosp & stated off the strength. W/M Capt PERRY Rawn proceeded on 14 days leave to the U.K. W/M No. M/019220 Pte BRACE R.S.C. M.T. Mot. Cyclist proceeded to duty with H. R. D. M. S. W/M	
	21/7/18		Instructions from A.D.M.S. Lt. THERON. R. Rawn to transferred & proballo C.F.D. Capt. HAWKINS. Rawn returned from leave & took over command of the unit. W/M	
	22/7/18			

Army Form C. 2118.

WAR DIARY
or
INTELLIGENCE SUMMARY.
(Erase heading not required.)

Instructions regarding War Diaries and Intelligence Summaries are contained in F. S. Regs., Part II. and the Staff Manual respectively. Title pages will be prepared in manuscript.

Place	Date	Hour	Summary of Events and Information	Remarks and references to Appendices
Fell	23/2/		Capt Macray J.R.S. Rawes reported his arrival from Ambala CFB & took over 10th the unit & is taken on the strength. Under instructions from ADMS Pte MORTON who relieves Cpl S Pritchard to Ambala CFB & Pte RANDAL 1st Hussars is Transferred duty 4762 unit from Ambala CFB. The following of unit's reported to ANC — by an escort of 1/1st Stuart No 1/0385338 Dr MURPHY L DSC HT No 1/376 Dr PITTS PE 1 GS Wagon & 4 PD Horses. Received notice of movement of the most forward post of ourselves at CHABOWRI. S.MS v SS. Used as OP. Ordered to proceed to attack at TORRAND. En-route to the post. Under instructions from ADMS. His enterum Fd Ambulance to transfer 12th unit. H.Q. Temporarily attached to this unit.	
			Sgt-Maj EDWARDS Return Cpl FARRELL " Pte POTTICE " PERRY " HICKS York & Lancs Regt	
	24/2/		S.B.S. RAFIUDDIN & No 14 Indian GS Pte WHEELER 4th Hussars Division, ordered to Cantonment from the Fuller L.F. O. Y & taken on strength by order to assume	

(Aj092. Wt W12639/M1293. 75 10 9. 1/17. D. D. & L., Ltd. Forms/C.2118/14.

WAR DIARY
or
INTELLIGENCE SUMMARY.
(Erase heading not required.)

Army Form C. 2118.

Place	Date	Hour	Summary of Events and Information	Remarks and references to Appendices
West.	23/6		Remainder of to unit entrained & left at Salaux for WAREELLES on Rail.	
		12.9 a.m.	Ambulance & M.T. personnel to Train No 3 at 10.30 p.m.	
			The horse transport & remained of personnel with Capt Hawkins left Train B at 1.37 a.m.	
		9.20 p.m.	Wagons & cacolets entrained & train B left Salaux 1.37 a.m.	
	25/6 to 8/6		The day & night quiet in the Train. Journey only interrupted for "Halte Repas" which station arrived & supplying of water & coffee at Hallt Repa at the following stations & the usual places.	
			NOGENT-sur-SEINE — 11.31 A.m.	
			LES LAUMES — 2.30 p.m.	
			MAS-PALAIS, MACON — 7.30 p.m.	
			MIRAMAS — 1.30 a.m.	
			Train enjoyed by Sadiste, O.P.R. & asst. H.P. Qusttistern & by St Landry. O.C. from Capt Hawkins. Arrived at MARSEILLES (at Sare Gare) at 7.33 p.m. 25th degno & furnish extreme in bon the on has arrived there to be met No 10 Rest Camp too into lorries provided C.T. transport were parted & camp about 10 mins, accommodation good.	

Signed: Skelcote Capt R.A.M.C.
Com 1 Div 1

COMMITTEE FOR THE
4 NOV 1919
MEDICAL HISTORY OF THE WAR

Shalsole Road. F. U.

R/R Cn. 2533.

Adjutant Confidential

War Diary
of
SIALKOT CAV. FIED AMBULANCE.

from 1.3.18 to 31.3.18

Vol. XXXVIII

Army Form C. 2118.

WAR DIARY
or
INTELLIGENCE SUMMARY.   Vol. XXXVII

(Erase heading not required.)

Instructions regarding War Diaries and Intelligence Summaries are contained in F. S. Regs., Part II. and the Staff Manual respectively. Title pages will be prepared in manuscript.

Place	Date	Hour	Summary of Events and Information	Remarks and references to Appendices
Field (Marseilles)	1/3/18		6 Mule Auxilary Cos. & at the Horse Transport Vehicle embarked on the H.T. "Invicta" & H.T. "City of Benares". The H.T. & M.T. personnel & animals returned to camp on completion of embarkation of vehicles.	
"	2/3/18		1 P Mule & 1 Indian Horse mechated coal & Sialkote Bn MPS & sailed off to attempt Ben & Camp temperature stealing under embarkation seed out as per ac.	
"	3/3/18		Drew khaki drill clothing & blankets to the British troops & pour for remain due at Marseilles dock.	
"	4/3/18		1 N.C.O. & 1 man A.S.C. M.T. of Superintendent A.F.A. went to meet party then arrived for attachment to the unit embarked at Gargoyle Forced Car the active Service.	
"	5/3/18		The unit received of Egypt. Capt Mackay Rouse in charge of all the British personnel of animals & 16 Indians & travel to H.T. "Java" to Capt. Howker Rouse & with 1 S.P.S. & 10 old O.R. a house to H.T. "Ellenga". Embarkation of unit Party completed at 18.00.	

Army Form C. 2118.

WAR DIARY
or
INTELLIGENCE SUMMARY.
(Erase heading not required.)

Instructions regarding War Diaries and Intelligence Summaries are contained in F. S. Regs., Part II. and the Staff Manual respectively. Title pages will be prepared in manuscript.

Place	Date	Hour	Summary of Events and Information	Remarks and references to Appendices
at sea	7/3/16		Convoy sailed from Marseilles harbour at 4 p.m. WHH	Dmo/1
"	8/3/16		at sea. WHH	
"	9/3/16		Touched Malta at 3 p.m. WHH	
"	10/3/16		Sailed from Malta 2 p.m. WHH	
"	11/3/16		at sea WHH	
"	12/3/16		" WHH	
"	13/3/16		" WHH	
"	14/3/16		" WHH	
Egypt.	15/3/16		Arrived at Alexandria at 2 p.m. WHH	
"	16/3/16		Men remained on board in Alexandria docks. WHH	Dmo/11
"	17/3/16		Men disembarked at Alexandria from H.T. "Ellenga" & H.T. "Suwanto" Arrival informed that the voyage was a this has no casualties but entrained at Alexandria for Tel-el-Kebir at 7 p.m. WHH	Dm II

WAR DIARY
or
INTELLIGENCE SUMMARY.

(Erase heading not required.)

Place	Date	Hour	Summary of Events and Information	Remarks and references to Appendices
Tel-el-Kebir	16/3/18		Unit arrived at Tel el Kebir at 1.15 a.m. Met at Tel Station & conducted to camp by representative from Mobile C.P.F. Sergt Churchill W.O. & J.C. Gideon R.R.J. reported to base having escorted the arrival to previous day. All M.O.S. & R.S.R.S. reported they ascud to Lt Col Forrest VMS A actg S.M.O. Tel el Kebir.	WAH
	19/3/18		H.T. & M.T. vehicles & M.T. personnel arrived at its camp from Port au Price. Had a conference of all the M.O.s of depot with the censor. Sent the S.M.O. O.C.s transport & others by [illegible] all the M.O.s & S.R.S.s of the Victoria Convoy Cobild (point 4) to inspect [illegible] 13th Sent the Stationary Hosp. & 168 Indian Field Amb & [illegible] etc. as given for each of the various corps to be given. The balances placed at the reception of sick & the Divisions with the exception of such Medical personnel of the Tank Brigade as field and of Parco as have arrived.	WAH
	20/3/18			

Army Form C. 2118.

WAR DIARY
or
INTELLIGENCE SUMMARY.

(Erase heading not required.)

Instructions regarding War Diaries and Intelligence Summaries are contained in F. S. Regs., Part II. and the Staff Manual respectively. Title pages will be prepared in manuscript.

Place	Date	Hour	Summary of Events and Information	Remarks and references to Appendices
Tel. el Kebir	21/3/16		Infantry Camp & Pumps Coys moved up to tent lines. Last batch of horses forwarded in 3 days draw from Cairo	
"	22/3/16		S.S. Rochdale Castle & H.T. Caird H.T. & Arcadia off. Signed for horses landed	WM
"	23/3/16		No. 11,021 Sadd. Sargent Hercof R.H.C. appointed Stationary Corpl. & struck off to strength	WM
"	24/3/16			
"	25/3/16		G.O.C. Egypt visited the camp & to meet J.F.	WM
"	26/3/16			
"	27/3/16		OC's regiments & CFD's to the Camp, ...to...headquarters on the occasion of the visit of the Duke of Connaught. H.R.H. Gen. Kitchener & C. Mitchell CFD &	WM
"	28/3/16 29/3/16		Capt. Hay & Lieut. Ramsey proceeded on 3 days leave to Cairo	WM

Army Form C. 2118.

WAR DIARY
or
INTELLIGENCE SUMMARY.
(Erase heading not required.)

Place	Date	Hour	Summary of Events and Information	Remarks and references to Appendices
Tel-el-Kebir	30/3/18		Phoenix - Swift Summers P.S.C.H.T. assured from Force & Expand the Unit.	
"	31/3/18		Capt Hawkins Rowe Expand from Lieu.	

W Hawkins
Capt Rowe

www.ingramcontent.com/pod-product-compliance
Lightning Source LLC
Chambersburg PA
CBHW080920230426
43668CB00014B/2164